Garden Ideas A to Z

By ELVIN McDONALD

An American Garden Guild Book

DOUBLEDAY & CO., Inc.   GARDEN CITY, NEW YORK

United States Department of Agriculture

George W. Park Seed Company

ALL ACROSS our land there is new awakening to the need of every individual to experience the beauties of nature. Gardeners and conservationists have known this for years, but it took the crusading efforts of Mrs. Lyndon Baines Johnson to make us all aware of what could be done when one person cared enough to plant a shrub, a tree, or a flower. In the planting there is faith. In the sprouting, hope. Growth brings enthusiasm. And that's how a good thing catches on. Neighborhoods and communities benefit. Where ugliness once spread its insidious depression, beauty grows instead.

And beauty is what this book is about. One plant in a pot, or an acre of wild flowers. One small deck for relaxing outdoors, or a sanctuary of berried trees and shrubs for bird-watching. A picturebook velvet lawn, or the tree of heaven managing to thrive on a city terrace. Wherever we are, this is the time for each of us to create our own unique places of beauty, and in this book you will find ideas to spark all kinds of planning and planting for indoors and outdoors.

I suppose I have been collecting garden ideas since at age three I transplanted a bean sprout from my mother's vegetable garden to a tin can of soil. The amazing thing is that this volunteer grew, and with some guidance draped a sunny window in our home that winter. By the time I was eight years old I was collecting gardening magazines, each of which sent my mind reeling with more ideas. I dug and built my own pit greenhouse. There was an iris garden with rhizomes counted and rearranged as often as my sons shuffle baseball cards. In the fall I might have one each of a hundred different tulips arriving in an exciting package from Holland. Or fifty cuttings of named begonias from correspondents in Kansas City. Daffodils grew from seed,

AZALEAS and rhododendrons, opposite, give welcome springtime flowers, with added bonus of evergreen foliage for color in all seasons. The franklinia, right, is a seldom-seen American native tree, a relative of the camellia, which it resembles. The creamy white blooms appear in summer.

3

and I busied myself learning how to cross-pollinate the roses.

Then came my discovery of the gloxinia in November of 1949. When my first gloxinias failed to prosper, I had the idea there should be an American Gloxinia Society patterned after the American Begonia Society, of which I had been a member since I was nine or ten years old. So I wrote a letter to *Flower Grower* (now *Home Garden*) magazine suggesting that anybody interested in forming such a society write to me. The editor, not knowing I was barely a teen-ager, published the letter. Hundreds wrote to me. So came *The Gloxinian*, a bimonthly magazine which I edited and published for the next ten years.

Since that first issue of *The Gloxinian*, I have been going through pictures of plants, flowers, and gardens. At first there were handfuls of prints, then hundreds. Finally, thousands. The occupational hazards are broken cuticle and bleary eyes. But still I go on searching for photographs that capture the deep feelings I have for the plants I grow, the gardens I plant, and the places I visit. As editor of *Flower and Garden* magazine, followed by several years with *The Floral Magazine* and the George W. Park Seed Company, I have had the unusual and enviable opportunity of traveling extensively to see and photograph gardens in nearly every state. More recently, in my present assignment as Garden Editor of *House Beautiful* I have traveled even more, with a new appreciation for landscape architecture and the fascinating historical aspects of plants and gardens.

I first gardened in the near-desert conditions of western Oklahoma with hardly a tree in sight. Then in Kansas City, Missouri, which by contrast is a gardener's paradise. I have twice been an apartment gardener in New York City, and today for the first time in my life I am gardening under trees on an acre near the north shore of Long Island. There are ideas in this book for all of these diverse gardens and climates I have known—and many more. Since I have three children—Mark, Steven, and Jeannene, ages ten, nine, and six, respectively—my current and greatest interest is in sharing the fun of gardening with them, and that is reflected in these pages too.

Ward Linton

4

As you read and use *Garden Ideas A to Z*, remember that I intended it as an idea book, something to inspire the beginning of a project that could lead you on a venture as far-reaching as my transplanting of a bean sprout. This is not a complete book of anything, but rather a collection of resources. Plant societies are listed in the appropriate places, and the list of seeds- and nurserymen will give you a place to buy virtually anything illustrated in these pages.

Without the dedicated garden photographers represented here, I could not have produced this book; my deepest respect and appreciation to all of them. Thanks also to my wife Edith, to my editor Ruth Buchan, and my associate Lawrence Power for the special ways they each helped make this collection of garden ideas possible.

—Elvin McDonald

New York City
1970

Colonial Williamsburg

ACHIMENES, opposite upper, grow from catkinlike rhizomes planted indoors in the spring, for blooms all summer, either in a bright window, or outdoors in a semishady spot. They come in many colors, and combinations, single- and double-flowered. Allamanda, opposite lower, is a tropical shrub with golden trumpet flowers and glossy evergreen leaves. In the North, grow it in a 20-inch tub which can be kept outdoors in warm weather, easily rolled inside for protection from frost. An arbor for rambler roses, above, is a feature of the Bryan garden at Colonial Williamsburg in Virginia. Boxwood is clipped into stylish topiaries, and as neat hedging to frame beds of periwinkle ground cover, through which bulbs thrust spring flowers.

Flower and Garden

Aₙₙᵤₐₗₛ—plant lots of them for a quick and sure abundance of flowers to cut all summer. Fortunately, the more you cut for arrangements indoors, the more they'll bloom outdoors. Sunset cosmos, above left, blooms early and long, forming bushy plants 2½ feet tall. Zinnias like the F_1 hybrids, above right, fairly zing with color. Poppies, of flamboyant hue and delicate petal, grow easily in a sunny, sandy site. The Iceland F_1 hybrid Champagne Bubbles, opposite upper right, unfurls huge flowers in myriad colors. The golden Mexican tulip-poppy, hunnemannia, yields three-inch flowers over a long season. Try it next to blue, blue larkspur or delphinium.

George W. Park Seed Company

ANNUALS will fill your garden with color from seed to bloom in sixty days. Try them, you'll be amazed. A sweeping border of blossom will be dazzling, and there'll be plenty of cutting material too. Plan any combination you like, monochromatic or multicolor. The zinnias, left, combine white, pink, and rose with a border of dwarf lavender asters. *Arctotis grandis*, upper right, is known as the blue-eyed African daisy. Use it in any sunny, well-drained site. First rosettes of feltlike blue-green leaves form, then bolt into bud with elegant long stems crowned by bluish-white flowers. Beautiful in the border and cut; the blooms close at night. It self-sows but is never weedy. Celosias like the Floradale hybrid, center right, provide vibrant color outdoors until frost. Use as fresh cut flowers. For winter bouquets air-dry by hanging bunches upside down in airy, dry, shaded place. The variety shown is of the crested cockscomb type. The plume or feather celosias come in an even wider color range and height selection. To succeed with celosias, start every year with new hybrid seeds; those saved from the garden revert to common pigweed quality. Nicotiana or flowering tobacco, lower right, blooms from early in the season until hard frost. *N. affinis*, and the hybrids Daylight and Sensation are scented at night. Use for bedding and cutting. Dwarf White Bedder is excellent for pots, either outdoors in summer container gardens, or indoors in a sunny window or greenhouse.

Roche

Bodger

Burpee

Bodger

ANNUAL bells-of-Ireland, below, grows 18-inch stems of bells; try in arrangements, fresh and green, or dried and pale beige.

ANNUAL asters: Grow them for mid- to late summer flowers. Beautiful in the garden; great for cutting. Cactus-flowered Massagno strain, above, has finely quilled petals; plants grow 24 inches tall.

ANNUAL Twinkles phlox, below, will carpet the ground with six-inch plants smothered by starry, white-edged, salmon pink flowers.

ANNUAL Fire Emerald gazanias, below, thrive in sun and heat. Try in pots for vivid patio color. Give seeds early start indoors.

ANNUAL Bright Butterflies snapdragons, below, are a new class with flared trumpets. Grow in masses for garden color and cutting.

Goldsmith

Bodger

Bodger

Bodger

Bodger

ANNUAL Tiger marigold, far left, blooms in eight weeks from seed, and keeps going for a long, long season; only hard freezing stops it. Tiger represents the French-type marigold, but is actually a new intergeneric hybrid between the French and African classes. Grows 12 inches tall, spreads to 15 inches wide. The flowers of *Didiscus caeruleus*, center left, are all "lace and lavender-blue" on slender stems for cutting. Needs moist, well-drained soil, and several hours of sun. F_1 hybrid marigold Golden Jubilee, left, grows uniformly and has a compact habit. Use it in the row to give the appearance of a neat, clipped hedge, about 20 inches tall. The Bright Butterflies snapdragons, upper left above, are available in mixture or by separate colors. The F_1 hybrid plants grow with vigor, to 30 inches. Try them for a long season of bloom; some plants may live over winter, behaving as perennials. Helianthus Sungold, upper right above, is a sunflower you won't have to look up to; it grows only 15 inches tall, and bears huge chrysanthemum-like flowers. Mexican sunflower or Fireball tithonia, lower left above, has velvety, glowing orange flowers that rise on stems from four to eight feet tall. The African daisy named dimorphotheca, lower right above, thrives in heat and sun, covering 12-inch plants with a carpet of flowers from June on.

ANNUAL amaranthus Early Splendor, below, has almost-luminous leaves from summer to frost; three feet tall.

Sakata

Pan-American Seeds

ANNUAL all-stars: petunias. Color range, bloom season, and growth habit make them tops, illustrated here by the Cascades: Pink above left and above in planter; Red below left.

ANNUAL cockscomb or crested celosia, above: Try planting in knot garden design for Persian carpet effect. Dahlias are easy to grow from seeds. Start indoors in February. Save tubers of favorites.

George W. Park Seed Company

BAMBOO is so strongly associated with the tropics, it is surprising the number of varieties that are hardy through winters far into the North. Moso bamboo, *Phyllostachys edulis*, right, is hardy to zero. Yellow-groove bamboo, *P. aureosulcata*, grows to 33 feet tall; survives temperatures to 20° below zero. Try as screening plants in Oriental or contemporary landscape plans. By contrast, pygmy bamboo, *Sasa pygmaea*, grows only 10 inches tall in sun or shade. Use it as a ground cover.

Morley Baer

AUTOMATIC watering pot called Plantender®, above, solves plant sitter problems and promotes better growth. A sensing device maintains correct soil moisture level, but the plant itself determines how much water is added to the soil. Look for other automated plant-care equipment coming on the market.

AVOCADO tree, right, makes a handsome house plant in bright light or full sun. Starting in water is not necessary, unless you have a youngster who would enjoy watching the root form. Otherwise, simply let seed dry a few days, then plant in a five-inch pot of soil; use equal parts garden loam, peat moss, and sand. Keep moist. After seedling begins active growth, feed every two or three weeks with liquid fertilizer. To start seed in water, submerge lower third in glass or jar; hold in place by inserting three toothpicks around the seed. When seed begins vigorous growth, transplant to soil as previously described. After a year of growth, an avocado makes a sizable indoor tree that will do well even in a city apartment.

Paul E. Genereux

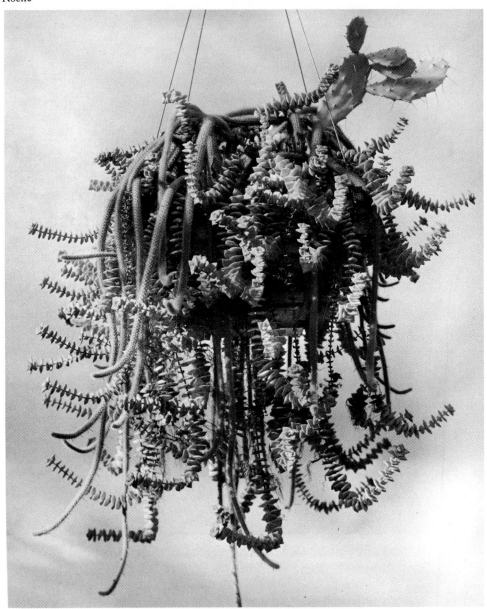

BASKET plants give eye-level beauty indoors or out. A basket that can take sun and heat, above, combines opuntia, *Crassula perfossa*, and *Aporocactus flagelliformis*. ·For a cool, shady spot, use blue or white browallia, left.

Paul E. Genereux

Roche

BASKET of fuchsias, above, blooms all summer in bright light or early morning sun. Try to situate fuchsias in the coolest part of your garden where they will be protected from hottest sunlight and drying winds. Fancy wandering Jew, *Tradescantia fluminensis variegata*, below, makes a ball of creamy-striped green leaves and white flowers. Grows well in filtered sun.

BASKET plants that will bloom in the shade cast by trees, roof overhangs, and lath houses, are much to be treasured. For this purpose, impatiens, above, is unsurpassed. Dwarf-growing Elfin is ideal for baskets, but any impatiens will do. Mix or match the colors. They all seem like jewels. In hot weather, baskets often need water twice a day. Feed weekly with diluted liquid fertilizer.

Roche

Roche

Maynard L. Parker

BEGONIA Cleopatra basket, above, sends up sprays of pink bloom in winter and spring; chartreuse and brown leaves are attractive all year. Other begonias for baskets: Anna Christine, Dancing Girl, Laura Engelbert, Lenore Olivier, *B. limmingheiana*, and Pink Parade. Use one large perfectly grown begonia like Houghtoni, left, as an accent plant. Or, by contrast, try grouping begonias with plants needing similar growing conditions. Silver bowl, opposite, holds angel-wing and rex begonias, aluminum plant, bromeliad, and grassy tuft of *Chlorophytum bicheti*.

Roche

Paul E. Genereux

BERRIED shrubs, and trees with ornamental fruit, give color to the garden in fall and winter, provide material for arrangements inside, and attract birds. Bittersweet, above left, has brilliant orange berries on female vines; a male pollinator is needed nearby. Colorful berries and fruits shown above right, beginning at top: hips of *Rosa hugonis*, highbush cranberry (*Viburnum trilobum*), yew, American holly, and *Cornus kousa*. Other shrubs with showy berries or fruit: bush honeysuckle, beautyberry or callicarpa (violet berries), cranberry cotoneaster, viburnums *opulus*, *tomentosum*, and *xanthocarpum*, rhodotypos, pyracantha, Oregon grapeholly, sea buckthorn, and snowberry. Trees with showy, long-lasting ornamental fruit include English and Washington hawthorn, Hopa crab apple, and European mountainash.

BIENNIALS like the velvety pansies above grow from seeds sown in late summer of one year and bloom the following spring and summer; then the plants die. Start the seeds in July or August in a cool, moist, well-lighted place such as on the north side of a wall or hedge; transplant to the border in September. Mulch with straw or leaves after freeze-up in late fall. For massing in beds, combining with spring bulbs, and in con- tainer gardens, use forget-me-nots, English daisies (bellis), cheiranthus (wallflower), vio-las and pansies. I have known pansies to blossom all winter in a cold but sunny walled garden and to cheerfully defy late spring snows in northern Minnesota. For border plant-ings, in combination with per-ennials, try canterbury bells, foxglove, sweet William, hes-peris (sweet rocket), lunaria (honesty or money plant), and verbascum. When sum- mer heat arrives, replace or interplant the early-flowering, cool-loving biennials such as English daisy and pansy, with annuals like petunias and ageratum. The larger and later-flowering kinds such as foxglove and sweet William will give a second round of bloom if the first crop is cut back before seeds ripen. When seeds are allowed to mature, many biennials will self-sow; all you have to do is watch for volunteers and thin them.

Gottscho-Schleisner

BIRDS bring life to the home garden and are a delight during the winter months. Attracting species like the nuthatch, above, to a window feeder requires special attention. Start feeding early in the fall so that, as the birds arrive, they include your feeder in their daily schedule of stopping places. Keep a regular supply of attractive food available all the time. Birds are fond of sunflower seeds, millets, and fats either as suet or in peanut butter or doughnuts. Remember, also, that dogs and cats are birds' least favorite companions. The bird-watcher's window, below, framed with house plants looks out on an environment planned for birds. The essential requirements of food, water, and cover are all provided in this sanctuary. Berried bushes give safe roosting at night, food and a place to perch in the daytime. Feeders have been built high above the ground; funnel-shaped metal guards on poles discourage squirrels from stealing food. Native trees give protection from predators. Water is provided by a running brook. If you are not fortunate enough to have a natural stream, use a rock garden pool, or birdbath.

Gottscho-Schleisner

BIRD OF PARADISE is a fantasy flower from the tropics that sends up exotic yellow, blue, and orange flowers in the winter from clumps of leathery, evergreen leaves. The common variety shown above, *Strelitzia reginae*, grows three to five feet tall. A dwarf form stops at 18 inches. The giant "bird," *S. nicolai*, grows slowly, but after a few years reaches 15 to 18 feet, and is suitable as an outdoor plant only in mild regions. As a container plant, pot bird-of-paradise in a 10- to 15-inch tub, and do not disturb for several years. Indoors, provide a sunny to partially shaded place, moderate temperatures (60–70°), a moist growing medium composed of equal parts garden loam, peat moss, and sand, and feed biweekly. Summer the plant outdoors on a terrace, patio, or other paved growing area. Young strelitzias, either seedlings or divisions, are not likely to bloom for at least four years, but the foliage makes an interesting accent in all seasons. In warm climates where frost seldom occurs, strelitzias may be planted in beds outdoors in any site from sun to shade. They thrive on a deep, rich, well-drained soil kept moist.

California Redwood Association

BONSAI, the Oriental art of dwarfing and shaping container-grown trees and shrubs, represents a deliberate slowing-down of plant growth. This requires extreme patience on the part of the gardener; first to learn the techniques that date from fourteenth-century Japan, and then to nurture the plants as faithfully as a pet. To anyone who has ever felt the pressures of our jet-away world it will come as no surprise that this peaceful pursuit has become a major diversion. Hardy trees and shrubs often cultivated as bonsai include cryptomeria, Japanese white pine, Dawn redwood, Heller Japanese holly, gray-bark elm, and flowering quince. These need winter temperatures, either buried in a sandy pit, or stored in a coldframe or cold greenhouse. Kinds suitable for bonsai work

Roche

that can be treated as house plants include pyracantha, dwarf pomegranate, common myrtle, gardenia, and small-leaved azaleas. When potted in classic bonsai containers, plants in all stages of training make fascinating displays. The redwood deck, above, serves as a convenient growing area on view from the house. *Cotoneaster horizontalis* in an asymmetrical shape, left, is positioned to one side of a hexagonally shaped pot to create a perfectly balanced relationship between plant and container. By contrast, balance for a symmetrical gardenia, right, is achieved by centering the trunk in a round container. If you are interested in dwarfing plants, write for more information to the American Bonsai Society, P.O. Box 95, Bedford, New York 10506.

Roche

BORDER of hardy perennials frames herringbone-brick walk in formal garden, opposite. The time is early summer with madonna lilies in peak bloom. Woven into these flowers, but not seen, are bulbs and plants for spring color, and for fall there will be asters, solidago, aconite, liatris, helenium, and early hybrid chrysanthemums. Sweeping curve gives excitement to border, above, where something is always blooming; here Oriental poppies steal the show, but with ample support from astilbe, columbine, daylily, oenothera, delphinium, peony, and lupine. Border updated to easy-care redwood planting bed, right, is resplendent with spring flowers of primroses, rhododendrons, and hydrangeas. Bark strip separates lawn from bed; simplifies mowing.

Phil Palmer

BOTTLE gardens can be a showcase for nature in miniature, or a place to propagate delicate plants that need high humidity. For a large bottle garden with a stopper like the one opposite upper, try miniature palm, fittonias, small ferns, and a young dracaena.

When moisture forms inside, open the bottle to dry out a few hours. The brandy snifter, above, includes a miniature caladium, three different selaginellas, and a tiny *Sinningia pusilla* with pale lavender slipper gloxinia flowers. A terrarium is another kind of under-glass garden, very much like a bottle planting. In the lower photo opposite, rex begonia leaves are being propagated in glasses of water and pots of vermiculite. When you try a glassed-in garden, select plants that do well in strong light, without any direct sun. Keep soil moist, but be careful not to add too much water since it has no way to drain. To put a seemingly large plant through a small bottle neck, wash away soil from roots, then coil a sheet of tissue paper around the plant until it can be slipped inside the bottle. Position by using wire tongs.

BOUGAINVILLEA, above right, is usually associated with great masses of color in southern gardens. For fun, try a young plant in a 5-inch pot. Keep pruned back to not more than 18 inches high in summer. The following winter the branches will be covered with colorful bracts.

BRIGHT blue is an unusual color in flowers, but that describes *Scilla peruviana*, lower right, a bulb to grow outdoors in mild climates. Try forcing in a pot, like a Dutch hyacinth in the North.

Harry Philpott

Paul E. Genereux

BROMELIADS are tropical plants without temperament. Year-round good looks, handsome blooms, and great tolerance to neglect characterize these members of the pineapple family. The display above shows varieties with leaf rosettes from one inch to nearly three feet in diameter. As with their familiar relative, Spanish moss, these bromeliads are air plants, and that is why a "tree" like the one shown can be made by covering the roots of such kinds as billbergias, aechmeas, and cryptanthus with osmunda fiber and wiring them to a piece of driftwood. The *Cryptanthus fosterianus*, left, has bronze-and-silver, zebra-striped leaves that swirl like a star.

Paul E. Genereux

Paul E. Genereux

BROMELIADS in bloom make an exciting show. The yellow flowers of *Aechmea pineliana*, upper left, grow from a scarlet cone of bracts. The leaves are copper-tinted gray and rose. *Billbergia leptopoda*, upper right, has small dark green, upright rosettes with slender recurved flower petals in blue and green in rose bracts. *Aechmea fasciata*, left, has sage-green leaves striped silver. The long-lasting flower head is rosy pink accented by bright blue florets. To force bloom from a mature bromeliad, enclose it for a few days in a polyethylene bag with a ripe apple. For information about the Bromeliad Society write 1811 Edgecliffe Dr., Los Angeles, Calif.

Paul E. Genereux

BULBS: They deserve to be used much more than they are for easy care and unusual blossoms. Instead of limiting yourself to the popular tulips and narcissus, try the crown imperial, *Fritillaria imperialis,* which responds to daffodil culture. Plant in fall in rich soil.

BULB for icy cool white-and-green summer flowers, ismene, below, needs spring planting in rich, moist soil.

Roche

BULB for surprising flowers in autumn, colchicum, below, is planted in August: leaves grow in spring.

Gottscho-Schleisner

Morley Baer

CACTI and other succulents can be used to create interesting plant groupings indoors and out. Jade plants (crassula) grow in matching earthenware pots, left, with rosettes of echeveria and mesembryanthemum in rock-mulched bed by steps. Tinted glass jug adds a pleasant touch. A collection of different hardy sempervivums, opposite, grows in a free-form design with stone and a small piece of Featherock® contrasting with a clump of *Festuca ovina glauca*. Sempervivums vary in color from grass-green to glaucous blue, bronze, and burgundy. Living stones with daisylike flowers, below left, grow well in shallow containers of sandy soil, mulched with stones selected to match as closely as possible the succulent plants. Paramount hybrid lobivopsis, below, gives a bouquet of pastel bloom in early summer. To receive information about the Cactus and Succulent Society of America, write to Box 167, Reseda, California 91335.

Larry B. Nicholson

Larry B. Nicholson

CALADIUMS have fancy leaves that give color in sun or shade, indoors or outdoors. Mrs. W. B. Halderman, left, combines pink, rose, and dark green. Plants of white-and-green Candidum, right, have been added in this terrace garden for the summer, to follow spring bulbs; they will also hide ripening daffodil foliage. Caladiums that are predominately white or light pink are especially effective in deeply shaded gardens. On the other hand, caladiums grow equally well in full sun, which is the exposure they have in Florida where they are propagated and grown in open fields. Use caladiums as container plants in pots, tubs, boxes, and baskets, or plant them directly in the ground outdoors. Start the tubers indoors in a warm place in February or March. Tubers planted rightside up will have larger, but fewer leaves; those planted upside down send up more clumps of leaves. Use a mixture of equal parts peat moss, vermiculite, and garden loam. Keep moist, warm (65–75°), and provide at least four hours of bright light, or grow them in a fluorescent-lighted garden. As soon as the leaves begin to unfold, transplant to individual pots; a six-inch size is fine at this stage whether the plants will eventually be planted directly in the garden, or used in a container. Fertilize with a liquid houseplant food once every two weeks. Near the end of the growing season withhold fertilizer and water. When leaves have dried up, remove, and store tubers in a dark, cool (55–65°) place until spring.

Paul E. Genereux

Gottscho-Schleisner

CHILDREN'S play area, opposite, includes swing, trapeze bar, and sandbox, with soft, no-maintenance surrounding surface of shredded bark. When children are older, sandbox can be used as a raised planting bed for flowers. Gourds, right, are favorites of young gardeners. Let your youngster sow the seeds outdoors where they are to grow after the weather is warm in spring. Situate near a wire fence or trellis on which the vines can climb. A packet of ornamental mixed gourds will yield shapes of orange, pear, egg, apple, penguin, and some warted. A few grape-hyacinth bulbs planted in a small tray, below, teach the art of forcing to a young gardener. Plant bulbs in early fall. Keep moist in a cool place (in the garage or outdoors in coldframe) until January. Then bring to a sunny, warm window. Keep moist. Blooms will be out in three or four weeks. The unguentine plant, *Aloe vera*, below right, fascinates children. Clear mucous in the leaves is valued for treating burns.

Robert Baur

Roche

CHILDREN will delight in growing Jack's beanstalk garden, left, by sowing beans and grass with an onion or two in plastic tray. Keep warm and moist in a bright place. "Mow" grass with scissors. Dish garden of wildings from floor of the forest, below, needs, a cool, bright, moist place indoors. Plants include princess pine, fern, goodyera, partridge berry, hepatica, and mosses. A morning glory in a pot, right, makes an exciting project because it grows so quickly. Sow three seeds in a five-inch pot of soil with thin bamboo stake. Keep moist in a sunny place. Note, these stems twine clockwise; some plants go in counter motion.

Gottscho-Schleisner

Roche

CHILDREN —of any age—will enjoy this project: A topiary of English ivy shaped to resemble an animal, bird, or geometrically stylized tree. Here the armature for a duck was made of eight-gauge iron wire (available at hardware store), then stuffed with moist sphagnum moss and thickly planted with rooted cuttings of Shamrock English ivy. Grow in sunny, moist, cool place.

Florida Citrus Commission

Larry B. Nicholson

CITRUS trees in dwarf form make outstanding house plants. They are characterized by glossy, dark, evergreen foliage; waxy, white, fragrant flowers; and highly decorative edible fruit year round. Culture indoors is simple: a warm, sunny place with moist soil and biweekly feeding. The remarkable thing is that both fruit and blossoms appear simultaneously, left. The Ponderosa lemon, above, makes the most spectacular show of all. It usually has at least one lemon in some stage of maturity. By harvest, the fruit on a 12-inch plant may weigh two pounds. The miniature orange or calamondin shown in an entry, right, has an abundant flower crop followed by one- to two-inch oranges of bright, glowing color, not just once but through most of the year. After the fruit begins to grow, it will practically cover a well-grown plant, and can be made into a delectable marmalade. In addition to the kinds shown, there are many other oranges and lemons available as true dwarfs, as well as tangerines and mandarins, grapefruit, limes, tangelos, and kumquats. Potted citrus trees were favorites of Louis XIV in his fabled orangerie. His gardeners forced bloom by removing plants from the soil and letting them dry out. The shocked plants were then bathed in milk and repotted, after which they are said to have produced an unbelievable profusion of bloom. You can grow your own orangerie and use it to decorate the outdoor living area in summer; in the winter it will make part of the house seem like a tropical retreat. Other plants you can grow indoors for edible fruit include Tiny Tim tomato, pineapple-guava (feijoa), guava, alpine strawberry, dwarf pomegranate, and dwarf banana.

Larry B. Nicholson

CITY gardens, poor things, must struggle with carbon monoxide, sulfuric acid, and all the other elements of air pollution. In addition, they often suffer a lack of sunshine. Since life for the city garden is so difficult, use only the hardiest plants and shrubs. Best trees include ginkgo, horse chestnut, hackberry, linden, poplar, sycamore, willow, and American ash. Shrubs that survive, even thrive in polluted air, include Oregon grape, rose of Sharon, burning bush, Cornelian cherry, pyracantha, mountain-laurel, andromeda, and Japanese holly. The ideal city garden provides a pleasant place to eat and entertain, and a spot to relax and read, while giving privacy and the sense of space. The garden on the other side of the fence, left, can't be any greener since it is an illusion created by mirrored cutouts which gives a feeling of beauty beyond. Curved brick planters of different heights in the same garden, above, use perspective to trick the eye and add depth. The high grape-stake fence offers protection as well as privacy. The light fixtures have been carefully integrated with the plantings to blend with the foliage during the day and highlight it at night. If you want a shield from hot sun and unwanted eyes, a vined trellis may be the answer.

CITY gardens share at least one feature—limited space. Effectively landscaping this urban garden required the tricks of perspective and selecting special materials to create an illusion of space. Curved walls, a disappearing path, two separate levels, and locust trees with light, airy foliage, give a feeling of openness and depth. Painting the rear wall white to match the low retaining walls in the foreground, leads the eye to the far end of the garden. Since city gardens are on view all year round, broadleaf and needle evergreens have been included in the plantings. Slate surfacing and easy-care shrubs keep the city garden looking well-groomed at all times. Random-shaped slate also adds a casualness of line needed to balance the austerity of surrounding high buildings. Interest can be added to a brick wall with espaliered trees or ornamental shrubs. In this garden the side wall has a dwarf apple espalier.

Gottscho-Schleisner

Gretchen Harshbarger George J. Ball

George W. Park Seed Company

COLOR in the garden at left is cued by the redwood fence which serves as a handsome backdrop for the border of Gloriosa daisies, marigolds, zinnias, and touches of blue ageratum. Spring bulbs precede the annuals, and low evergreens give winter color. Like snow in summer, the white sweet alyssum above is a stark contrast between the lawn and dark-hued coleus, and this is a good lesson in color: Very light colors illuminate the dark coloring of a plant like coleus. For rich color in the garden, plant a bed of salpiglossis Splash, right. This new F_1 hybrid thrives in climates where salpiglossis never grew before. Start the seeds early indoors, as for petunias.

51

Maynard L. Parker

COLOR combinations, successfully planned, provide great pleasure in gardening. A strong color scheme is used for the small flower bed, opposite, which is on view both from the house and the terrace. The sunny colors of crocus, daffodils, and yellow hyacinths in spring are followed by lemony petunias and zinnias in summer; chrysanthemums bloom until frost. Color, texture, and form work together in courtyard, above. Grassy liriope, gray santolina, and caladiums frame topiary trees. Delicate vine traces design on brick wall. For a garden with lots of color in one season, right, dogwood trees, rhododendrons, and azaleas are used.

Gottscho-Schleisner

Lord & Burnham

COLOR under glass every month of the year: You can make this dream come true even in a four-by-eight-foot lean-to like the one above. This small greenhouse with a lightweight aluminum frame is mounted on wooden timbers so that it can be dismantled and taken by the owners if they should move. Larger greenhouse, designed as a sunroom extension of the house, right, has concrete foundation. Color is provided by a geranium tree, baskets of browallia and bougainvillea, and chrysanthemums.

54

COLOR abounds in this home greenhouse, photographed in the peak of late winter flowering. Ruffly, rosy azaleas bloom for many weeks in the sunny, cool, moist, and airy atmosphere, along with cerise geraniums, red-and-white gloxinia (placed high for greater warmth), pink amaryllis, and wax begonias. Daffodils and fragrant freesias, forced into early bloom, enhance the more permanent flowering plants of chrysanthemums and creamy poinsettias, with chartreuse coleus in the foreground. Long-range planning is what it takes to have nonstop bloom in a home greenhouse.

CONTAINERS of geraniums, daffodils, azaleas, and amaryllis bring traditional plants into a contemporary setting, above. In the foreground, a slate
terrace and table; beyond, no-maintenance gravel on which to display potted
plants; and in the distance, a nearly-wild garden of azaleas, rhododendrons,
and evergreens. Potted plants to decorate this area are cultivated in another
place and brought here as they bloom.

Maynard L. Parker

CONTAINER gardens bring out the showmanship in a gardener, as evidenced above in modular shelves that shadowbox pots of succulents on a patio. The terracotta fish holds an aloe. Equally interesting in this kind of arrangement would be a collection of tuberous-rooted begonias, fuchsias, or geraniums, in contrasting foliage types and growth habits. Large hydrangeas in full flower, left, with frilly double petunias, grow in matched Italian terracotta pots. Container plants need an abundance of water at all times to keep growth luxuriant and fresh. Feed biweekly with a liquid houseplant fertilizer.

Gladys Diesing   57

Inside or out, impatiens, above, bloom nonstop. Miniature orchids, below, grow in three-inch pots.

CONTAINERS of cyclamen, like the one above, will bloom for months in four or five hours of sun (or in a fluorescent-lighted garden). Keep cool and moist.

Calla-lily begonia, above is a semperflorens type. Name derives from young all-white leaves furled like a calla. For pots, baskets, boxes, and tubs.

Pentas, above, bloom all year in sunny, airy window. Kohleria, below, needs dappled sun, moisture.

Regal or Lady Washington geraniums, right, make handsome container plants in all seasons; flowers winter, spring.

California Redwood Association

CONTAINER plantings and decks go together naturally. Portable trees and flowers enhance the outdoor living space, at the same time the deck serves as a display-growing area. Chrysanthemums are used in redwood planters, above. In the spring they are replaced by pots of pansies and tulips; petunias and nicotiana give summer color and fragrance. A low juniper is used in the foreground tub; matching tubs hold Japanese maples near the wall. Never underestimate the power of repetition, as evidenced by identical pottery planters, right. In a contemporary entry the avant-garde arrangement suits the overall design, but conventional plants soften the effect and add welcome color. Also dramatic would be a surfaced entry area with a geometrical arrangement of nine 10-inch clay pots filled with French marigolds.

Architectural Pottery

CONTAINERS give the gardener a chance to show off favorite plants when they are at the peak of bloom, or when the foliage is most colorful. An architecturally styled planter, left, adds another dimension of beauty. Standard redwood planters sold at local garden centers serve a practical purpose but they are not interesting from a design viewpoint. Try designing and building some of your own, with favorite plants in mind. The azalea shown is in complete unity with the Oriental-influenced stand and planter-box. Italian terracotta pots of azaleas and hyacinths marching up entry steps, below, may be used all year with different flowers by the gardening buff, or only on special occasions.

Al Blake

Western Wood Products

Decks make enticing entry and dining areas. The one above uses geraniums and metal sculpture to accentuate the clean lines of the house. The deck, left, incorporates a storage area in its design.

DECKS should use scale, style, and materials which work in relation to surroundings, existing landscaping, and wind and sun exposure. The two-level deck, above, gives additional space on a hilly location. It has a natural screening of trees so that high walls are unnecessary. Note the interest created by running the boards of the upper deck at an angle. A parquet effect is produced in the deck, left, by the use of short redwood pieces laid in alternate groupings. Try leaving out a square for a planting pocket.

Roc

DECORATIONS give the garden a focal point necessary for good design. Don't settle for the commonplace. Find a choice decoration, something you will cherish. The armillary sundial, above, is a natural for a sunny herb garden of thyme, mint, stachys, rosemary, and lemon verbena, with bricks set in herringbone pattern. In the dooryard garden, right, a Ming porcelain vase serves as an elegant holder for a birdbath, with ground cover of English ivy, Croesus and Enchantment lilies, and a Japanese maple tree. A Polynesian mood has been created in the small garden, opposite page, by the arrangement of the bamboo fountain and fence with the carved driftwood head. Plant materials include variegated Algerian ivy (*Hedera canariensis*) espaliered on the bamboo, with containers of geraniums, ferns, and calla-lilies at the sides, and cyperus, festuca, and alyssum in the foreground, all pleasingly arranged with stones.

Espaliers like the crab apple above have height and width but not much depth. This fan-shaped espalier softens the garage baffle on which it is trained, providing foliage, flowers, and fruit in season. *Deutzia gracilis* grows at the base. Enter right, the tailored vine: honeysuckle tamed to the pattern of a wooden screen designed to give a feeling of privacy without darkening rooms. Grassy liriope grows at the foundation. Pyracantha is equally suited to training in this manner. It has foliage all year, white flowers in spring, and bunches of brilliant orange and scarlet berries in fall and winter.

66

Jeannette Grossman

ENGLISH IVY forms an arresting pattern on a redwood fence, above, with wires stretched taut to train and hold the design. The *Clematis montana*, at far end of the fence, blooms in early spring. Heathers grow in the strip between fence and drive. Traditional espaliers, like the pear in a palmette verrier, left, can be trained in formal patterns or in free-form designs. Which you choose will depend on the architecture and the plant material. For large expanses of wall (six to fifteen feet), these plants are suggested: bearberry, *Caragana arborescens lorbergi*, purpleleaf filbert, winged euonymus, common fig, forsythia, Burford Chinese holly, *Jasminum nudiflorum*, star magnolia, crab apples Dorothea and Red Jade, and pyracantha. For low espaliers (three to eight feet), try Chinese redbud, flowering quince, spreading cotoneaster, and convexleaf Japanese holly. Dwarf espalier plants (one to four feet) include rock cotoneaster, Heller Japanese holly, Sargent juniper, and dwarf Japanese yew. For an espalier in a large tub, try Japanese camellia, Chinese hibiscus, or citrus.

Paul E. Genereux

67

Jeannette Grossman

Roche

EVERGREENS offer more potential for the garden than any other group of plants. In needle and broadleaf form there is unbelievable variety in growth habit and leaf coloring. Visit local nurseries and botanical gardens to learn what is being grown in your own area. Study nursery catalogs for other possibilities. If you have a high foundation to hide, try using one variety of low evergreen in

Paul Kohl

combination with one or two accent shrubs and trees. This helps avoid the usual dot-dot-dash effect of typical mixed evergreen foundation plantings. Use evergreens as patio screens for climate control and privacy. Plant evergreens in a sweeping curve as a dramatic backdrop for a flower border. Use pots of junipers trimmed to topiary or ming shapes in formal areas. If you live in the U.S.D.A. Plant Hardiness Zone 8,* or in a warmer climate, camellias will be your first love among broadleaf evergreens. If you are adventuresome and live in Zone 7, try camellias in high, light shade of tall pines, far left. While it is young, Scotch pine, left, makes a pleasant contrast with tall-bearded iris and lupines. When the tree crowds out the perennials, replace them with a sculptured boulder (lightweight Featherock® is easier to manage than a real boulder), and evergreen ground cover such as Baltic ivy. Every front yard does not have to be a lawn maintained with painstaking care. In the entry area above, the interesting planting of evergreens consists of heathers, pines, junipers, and creeping cotoneaster.

* To obtain a copy of the Plant Hardiness Zone Map, send twenty cents with your request for Miscellaneous Publication No. 814 to the Superintendent of Documents, U. S. Government Printing Office, Washington, D.C. 20402.

Gottscho-Schleisner

Fences can shelter from sun and wind, give privacy, or just add a decorative touch. Analyze your needs carefully to ensure choosing the right fence for your location. Unity of design with your house and plantings should be considered, as well as the physical requirements of the fence. The unassuming, yet completely effective screen of redwood strips, opposite, will in time be covered by vines of fragrant honeysuckle. The curved bench of the same material gives unity and a shaded sitting area. The brick wall surrounding the patio, upper right, cuts the wind on a hilltop. The delightful sight and sound of water is provided by a small fountain cut into the concrete surface. The rustic fence, center right, supports rose and crapemyrtle bushes and completes the uniquely American look of a California ranch house. A traditional white picket fence, lower right, is the perfect border for the formal plantings of boxwood hedges and tulips in a Colonial Williamsburg garden.

Maynard L. Parker

Gottscho-Schleisner

FERNS used indoors or outdoors add a touch of opulence to plantings. Their strong structural quality and marvelous texture set them apart wherever they are used. Ferns need little help from other plants in order to be effective. Simple plantings are definitely in order. However, this does not prevent them from having functional applications either as focal points, backgrounds, or as filler among other plants. The lichen-covered millstone walk, right, has been dramatized by beds of hardy ferns. The centers of the stones have been planted with thyme (*Thymus serpyllum albus*). Maidenhair ferns have been used as a low-maintenance border along the stone wall, left. They are sheltered from strong winds by the wall, and from strong sun by shade trees. Both these pictures show ferns in rustic, woodland settings, but in an antique or contemporary container a fern is totally sophisticated and can set a rich tone for any garden, patio, or room. With 10,000 varieties to choose from, you will have no problem finding a fern which will suit your esthetics and at the same time, fit special growing conditions. The north side of buildings and areas shaded by trees are generally best for sun-shy ferns which will thrive in moist, well-drained soil. Try using low-growing varieties to outline flowering plants for a natural bouquet effect. For information about the American Fern Society, write Mr. LeRoy K. Henry, Division of Plants, Carnegie Museum, Pittsburgh, Pa. 15213.

Paul E. Genereux

Roche

FRUIT trees, like the dwarf Bonanza peach, top, are especially showy when boxed in redwood.

Gᴇʀᴀɴɪᴜᴍs add foliage color, particularly when they are the fancyleaf varieties, above left. Old-fashioned and lovely, they have a new look when placed in a contemporary container, all uniform in size and hue.

74

GRASS rustling in the wind gives a pleasant sound and movement to the garden. When allowed to grow freely within a confined area, the natural, casual beauty be- comes a pleasant diversion from the stylized plantings of a cultivated landscape.

GROUND COVERS and bricks form a dramatic design, opposite. Juniper in prostrate form grows in background. Left pocket is *Sempervivum arachnoideum*, the cobweb houseleek, with summer flowers of rose-red. *Sedum cauticolum*, which has red flowers in autumn, grows in upper right pocket. Neatly edged, but otherwise untrimmed zoysia grass grows in foreground; any dwarf pink (dianthus) could be used for the same grassy effect, but with flowers in season. Ground-covering pachysandra, above, serves practical purpose in area that would be difficult to mow, and by contrast in texture with lawn and paving, gives strong emphasis to serpentine design. Right angles of redwood bench make it literally and figuratively a stopping place among the exaggerated curves: a deceptively simple element in a masterfully planned landscape. With growth, dogwood tree will assume increasing importance as a focal point.

Paul E. Genereux   Gottlieb Hampfler

GROUND COVERS give
lightness to shaded garden,
above left: The pale green
and creamy white leaves of
goutweed or aegopodium
grow naturally with the vis-
ually light and lacy ferns. De-
pendable, always-the-same
pachysandra, upper right, as-
sumes new interest when in-
terplanted with spring-flowering scilla, the leaves of which

can be removed as soon as
they begin to yellow in early
summer. Try daffodils and
snowdrops (galanthus) in
combination with pachysandra, English ivy, or Vinca
minor ground cover. Carpeting succulents and Korean
grass make a fascinating low-
upkeep entry garden, opposite
upper, extending to meet
steps and out to the street.

Mondrian-influenced paving
design, opposite lower, makes
a stunning effect by combining paving blocks with blue-
green tufts of Festuca ovina
glauca, leafy clumps of Aga-
panthus africanus (lily of the
Nile), and tiny-leaved ribbons
of dichondra (thyme could be
used in cold climate) which
boldly emphasize the clean
lines.

78

HEDGES are the answer to many landscaping problems. Use them to frame the garden, to assure privacy, as fencing, to screen a bad view, or as a baffle to cut down noise and dust from a busy street. Different hedges may be evergreen, deciduous, clipped, unclipped, flowering, or berried, and from 18 inches high to 15 feet. A hedge of flowering hydrangeas, left, makes a beautiful sight through arch, with taller privet hedge as screen in background. Trimmed boxwood hedges outline beds of jonquils, above, in a Colonial Williamsburg garden where billows of older untrimmed boxwood grow along the property line. Clipped privet hedge, opposite, frames a terrace and gives emphasis to the pinks and sedums that grow between paving stones. Pachysandra circles the tree.

Gottscho-Schleisner

Gottscho-Schleisner

81

HERBS need a sunny site and well-drained soil. In return they provide interesting plants of diverse sizes, shapes, and growth habits. Most are useful for fragrance and flavoring. If herbs have a common fault, it is that they prosper into unruly, weedy-looking plants. Control them by organizing contrasting shapes and colors into neat beds, firmly outlined by bricks, cobblestones, ceramic tiles, or redwood. In June, the herb garden at left is filled with the sweetness of madonna lilies, spicy pinks, a burgeoning bed of lavender, allium in full bloom, and the white daisies of feverfew. Potted geraniums accent the artifact, with yew on either side. The John Blair garden at Colonial Williamsburg, above, is a perfect example of the well-kept herb garden, with walks and beds cleanly detailed by bricks, and boxwood hedging for year-round color. Industrial ceramic piping, right, forms the design of this contemporary herb garden. The containers hold thriving communities of thyme, mint, bedstraw, lavender, rue, and Egyptian onions.

Paul E. Genereux

Malcolm R. Kinney

California Redwood Association

INDOOR gardens bring us close to nature. A single plant or a grouping like the ones here can change the entire mood of a room. There is that encouragement about new green leaves, that moment of excitement when you find a flower sheath on the cattleya, and the joy of seeing your own gloxinias burst into bloom. All this, plus the satisfaction of tending a garden indoors that depends solely on you for water, fertilizer, and a friendly atmosphere. A bay window in full sun with a thin curtain screening out strongest rays, above, provides a home for African violets in bouquets of bloom, orchids in variety—cattleya, cymbidium, and paphiopedilum—and hoya vines. The entry planter box of redwood, left, is spotlighted from above, and receives strong reflected natural light. Plants include English ivy, grape-ivy, philodendron, and ficus. If you have an east or west window, or partially shaded south window, try planting a "tree" as in picture opposite. Pots of coleus, odontoglossum orchids, philodendron, scindapsus, and caladiums are wrapped in sphagnum moss and tied to a piece of driftwood. African violets, columneas, and episcias also would grow well this way.

Gottscho-Schleisner

INDOOR gardens thrive when plants are grouped naturally, as if they were outdoors. This not only makes plants give a more vivid impression in a room, but the togetherness helps create a microclimate where increased humidity promotes better growth. A jungle garden is suggested, left, by the treelike dracaena and Chinese hibiscus, underplanted with diverse foliages in handcrafted pottery containers. A waterproof copper tray, raised slightly off the carpeting to permit air circulation, and filled with moist gravel, makes the planting possible. Plants include aglaonema, maranta, cycas, Fluffy Ruffles and polystichum ferns, aralia, citrus, and croton. A completely different mood is created in the garden room, above, where palms and a weeping fig (*Ficus benjamina*) suggest an eighteenth-century bower. English ivy thrives in the windows, in season encircling pots of flowering plants; here the time is winter, and rosy cyclamen bloom next to the cool panes. Summer brings pots of warmth-loving achimenes and gloxinias, and for autumn, chrysanthemums and kalanchoes. A grouping of marantas, ferns, and philodendrons at floor level completes the gardenlike setting. Translucent windowshades diffuse direct sun, and benefit plants.

Window Shade Manufacturers' Association

JAPANESE gardens are based on an imagery, tradition, and superstition which is difficult for the Occidental mind to grasp. But it seems the need for studied, simple beauty and quiet sanctuary in our complicated modern life has brought them great popularity. Ideally, a Japanese garden links both natural and man-made elements to create either a scene or mood. The secret of success is restraint. Since a whole philosophy of meditation and contemplation revolves around the Japanese garden, study and careful planning are required to adapt the concept. Line, mass, and texture in perfect relationship should create a central theme around which the entire garden is designed. Don't overplant or clutter with bits and pieces of sculpture. Use color with discretion. Keep to soft tones. Sand, which is traditionally used to represent water, has been raked, upper right, to swirl around partially submerged rocks. Rocks are used not to simulate nature but as pieces of sculpture. A border of evergreens and a few flowers are used to show the quiet passing of the seasons. Many of the basic elements of shibui—water, polished and rough stones, a lantern, and simple reeds—appear in the Japanese garden, far right. If wind makes the use of sand impractical, and you do not have natural water flowing on your property, try using mechanical methods. The pump for the small pool and stream edging the terrace, lower right, has been cleverly hidden by stones.

Jeannette Grossman

Roche   Max Tate

KALE with highly colored leaves and ornamental cabbage make interesting plants for pattern gardens, planted directly in the ground, or used in pots for accent. Plant seeds in late spring or early summer. Pot up or plant out when seedlings are still young. Feed and water through the summer. Spray often to keep pests from chewing up the leaves. With first cool days of autumn the plants change to beautiful colors. They stay attractive until severely cold weather. Bring potted specimens inside to enjoy for several more weeks after frost.

LANDSCAPING when handled with discerning taste often appears deceptively simple. The garden, right, has successfully translated pure Japanese into the Western garden idiom. Its quiet beauty is neither superficial nor accidental. This almost-shy garden hides many of the most important basics of good landscape design. All the elements have distinctive beauty and yet combine homogeneously into one unit of great subtlety: a redwood fence for privacy, black-eyed Susans for color, the soft geometrics of old brick for pattern, a disc-shaped pool for water, and a pine tree for shade. The three-tiered stand is a superb container for displaying succulents. Water-washed white stones are a true sculptural grouping. The moss-covered mall and English ivy border keep maintenance at a minimum.

Morley Baer

Gottscho-Schleisner

LANDSCAPING is the art of organizing outdoor space so that it is esthetically pleasing and functional as in the outdoor eating area, above. Form follows function in this *intime* patio. A vine-covered trellis shades daytime dining and a dwarf juniper adds interest to the concrete surfacing material. As here, beautiful landscaping involves more than growing beautiful flowers: it requires imagination, an eye for design, and a sense of style. Consider flowers, shrubs, and trees as they will look during all seasons in both youth and maturity. Within the framework of the topography and property lines, strive for a strong sense of design balanced with the fundamentals of easy maintenance and livability. Minimize defects; play up the strong points of the landscape.

The play area, left, makes excellent use of a single large curve to give a grand sweep to the lawn and at the same time keep the upkeep down. An edging material bordered by brick tile makes trimming unnecessary. Since the stand of grass is unbroken by plantings, mowing time is reduced and the size of the lawn magnified.

Maynard L. Parker

This inviting entry area has added interest because of the serpentine-curved walk of rough brick. Clever use of plantings of red and white azaleas and rhododendrons gives proportion to an irregularly shaped house. A columnar evergreen shelters the bay window from full view and, combined with deciduous shrubs, balances the plantings. The Ponderosa pine fence was chosen with neither privacy nor protection in mind. It is simply an attractive statement of the fact that the yard has come to an end. Its placement at an angle unifies the entire design.

Western Wood Products

The curve of this disappearing path adds illusion and mystery to the garden. It meanders out of sight and uses perspective to give a sense of space. A gnarled apple tree limits the sight line and leaves the viewer's imagination free to conjure the delights beyond. The secret of this technique is to create a point of focus in the background. Here a patch of friendly daffodils leads the eye past the tree; in other seasons, potentilla, oenothera, or hosta might serve as a focal point.

Gottscho-Schleisner

LANDSCAPING techniques of repetition and contrast are expertly handled in the patio, left. White double petunias in matched terracotta pots cleanly delineate the defined garden from the dense foliage beyond. Repetition is used again in white terry cloth pillows which counter the rough stone and concrete of the bench base. A hexagonal fire pit has been converted into an artful focal point. The distinctive stone statue is perfectly at home among succulents carefully arranged on white sand. A circular basin of water, with colored glass balls of varying sizes, resembles a bubbling fountain.

LIGHTS make it possible to have a garden indoors where little or no natural daylight reaches. There are presently two standard setups: One consists of two 20-watt fluorescent tubes in a 24-inch reflector, the other of two 40-watt tubes in a 48-inch reflector. Burn these 14 to 16 hours out of every twenty-four. Units designed for growing plants come with stands that may be adjusted to various heights, depending on the kinds of plants grown. Usually 24 inches is the maximum distance practicable from tube to the surface on which plants will be placed; 12 to 18 inches is desirable for most kinds. Fluorescents are not helpful to plants growing out of this range. Most units for gardening under lights are essentially utilitarian; they are ideal for use in a basement or spare room. One attractive application of fluorescent light for growing plants is to install the fixtures in some kind of bookcase arrangement, above, where luxuriant and colorful plants blend harmoniously with fine books, recordings, art objects, and a component music system. In the shelf shown, two 40-watt fluorescents concealed by a valance light flowering African violets and rhizomatous begonias. For information about the Indoor Light Gardening Society of America, write Mrs. Fred D. Peden, 4 Wildwood Road, Greenville, South Carolina 29607.

LIGHTING at night adds a new dimension of usefulness to the home landscape. Illuminate walks and steps for safety. Add fixtures to extend "daylight" in the outdoor living area and to cast light in the garden where you want to do nighttime planting. Install ample electrical outlets outdoors for powering equipment such as an edger, hedge trimmer, or mower. A dark green mushroom shade, opposite, casts light on geraniums and wax begonias in an entry garden. By day the perennial border, above right, reveals a massed shrubbery backdrop for an array of flowers. By night the same planting, center right, takes on more excitement, with spots on important trees and clumps of flowers—in all a pleasing picture from the terrace. Outdoor lamps styled like fanciful flowers, below, dramatically light fountains and trees.

General Electric

General Electric

General Electric

97

LILIES are the most spectacular of the hardy, summer-flowering bulbs—and if you meet their simple requirements, they are the easiest to grow. In the perennial border they can be planted in variety for flowers from May to September; earliest is *Lilium rubellum*, latest *L. auratum*. In between, June brings the Mid-Century hybrids such as Enchantment, Destiny, and Cinnabar, followed by the June-into-July Harlequin hybrids, *L. croceum*, and *L. szovitsianum*. Next come the great trumpets like Moonlight, Emerald Isle, and Green Dragon; Backhouse and Paisley hybrids; Aurelian hybrids; and *L. japonicum*. Black Dragon opens cool white flowers with purple on the petal reverses in late July and August, joined by *L. tigrinum flaviflorum*, which goes into September. August brings the elegantly beautiful *L. speciosum* hybrids, closely followed by, or sometimes at the same time with *L. auratum*, or hybrids that combine both groups. The all-white garden, upper right, features summer phlox with the magnificent Emerald Isle trumpet lily. All lilies make superb cut flowers, and the large size of most lends them to lavish casual displays. Moonlight, with its palest green-tinted yellow flowers, right center, is enhanced by the accompanying bells-of-Ireland. Lilies are equally valuable in any garden whether it is nearly-wild, as the setting for Aurelian hybrids, lower right, or strictly formal.

98

Oregon Bulb Farms

LILIES today represent tremendous hybridizing advances, made largely from species that a few years ago were grown only by collectors. For example, the Harlequin hybrids, above, were derived from the simple little *L. cernuum*. In this improved form, these Turk's-cap lilies measure four inches in diameter, and as many as twenty flowers are carried on one stem. Plant lily bulbs in spring or fall. They need a humusy, rich, moist soil, perfectly drained, and at least a half day of sun.

Star Roses

MINIATURE plants need to be seen at close range to be appreciated. A collection of six different succulents, left, will fit on any small shelf or sill where they have a few hours of sun. Garden, below left, grows in tray elevated on pedestal so that tiny roses can be seen. Bo-Peep miniature rose, below, is shown with key for scale. Outstanding flowering miniatures for indoor gardens are *Sinningia pusilla* and other little gloxinias; they don't need much sun to bloom, and for necessary moisture you can grow them in a terrarium.

Narcissus *scaberulus*, upper right, is smallest daffodil in the world. Pot up bulbs in autumn; keep moist; winter over in cool garage or coldframe. Bring to flower in sunny, warm place in spring.

Orchids thrive in window wardian case, lower right. Wet gravel over radiator increases humidity.

PATIOS provide an inviting place for relaxing, entertaining, and dining
outdoors any time the weather is pleasant. Comfortable, well-designed,
weather-resistant furniture, ample lighting, and a sandbox for the children add to the appeal of the wooden patio deck above. It also serves as a
showplace for displaying container plants when they are at best. Here the spot-
light is shared by golden chrysanthemums and velvety red gloxinias.

The compelling outdoor living area shown opposite is a pocket of privacy protected from sun and wind, neighbors, and even noise—the pool has a splashing
fountain that masks out unpleasant sounds. The wooden patio deck serves as
an attractive and practical surface, with space for displaying container-grown
flowers. The wooden lattice overhead creates the pleasant illusion of dappled
sunlight, but at the same time serves as welcome protection from the heat
of summer. The delicate tree gives life to summer breezes. Beyond, an area
for sunbathing.

Gottscho-Schleisner

PATIOS and terraces provide all the pleasures of being indoors and outdoors at the same time. The two shown here reflect great contrast. Moss-covered squares of coral rock and a canopy of old trees, above, form an idyllic setting for dining alfresco. The here-and-now terrace, left, could be built in a few hours. Lay concrete blocks on sand. Use redwood table and benches. Add umbrella for shade. Utilitarian fence is quick way to have privacy while trees and shrubs grow.

Cotton Council

PATIOS in contemporary styling play up comfort. A canvas-awning canopy, above, can be tilted to cast a 10-foot circle of shade where it's needed at any given time. Cantilevered arm eliminates obstructing uprights. Round table with colorful mosaic tiles repeats shape. Seating is provided by cushions and a curving wooden bench along the patio edge. Tall fence in background screens unpleasant view, gives privacy, and protection from wind. At the same time the translucent panels have a welcome lightness and illusionary see-through quality. Canvas awning can be used to shade the outdoor living area in summer, left, then stored for winter to allow sunlight to come inside. Note use of citrus tree in container that can be moved inside during cold weather.

Cotton Council

Tritoma, below, blooms from June on, in red, white, and yellow combinations. Growth habit is like daylily, to three feet.

George W. Park Seed Company

PERENNIALS like those in the garden opposite multiply and bloom year after year. This easy-care border has drifts of snowy Shasta daisies, spikes of purple liatris, lemon daylilies, and bouquets of orange Enchantment hybrid lilies. Use variegated hostas, opposite lower, to add light in a shaded garden. They are effective edgers, and fine mixers, especially with ferns. Penstemons open spikes of bloom, above, in heather colors June through August. Recommended: the Viehmeyer hybrid penstemons. Tall-bearded iris, like Grand Alliance, left, highlight midspring gardens; select other iris for blooms April to fall.

Paul Kohl

PERENNIALS bloom from earliest spring until the last frost in fall. *Helleborus niger* even promises winter bloom. The great challenge is achieving bloom when and where you want it, and in the right color combinations. When planned successfully, the perennial garden is like a marvelous tapestry that is never the same but always beautiful. In the garden opposite, daylilies, iris, anchusa, dictamnus, and achillea give May bloom. A garden that features one plant has other rewards. The classic iris garden, above, is like a rainbow for one month every year. Iris are also important in contemporary container gardens, right, where the foliage contrasts boldly with architectural details.

Phil Fein

Gottscho-Schleisner

PERENNIAL belamcanda, above left, is an ideal plant. August blooms are followed by seeds in showy clusters like blackberries. Easy to start from seeds in the spring; some will bloom first year. *Delphinium cardinale*, above right, occurs naturally on California foothills and mesas. Elsewhere it is most unusual. It grows readily from seeds planted in early spring in a mixture of sand and loam. The bundles of stout roots that form on seedlings should be allowed to mature, and given a late summer dormant period. Plant roots out in early spring in full sun or very light, high shade. Provide coarse soil.

George W. Park Seed Company

Nelson Groffman

PERENNIAL water-lilies, left, come in hardy, tropical, and miniature varieties. (The tropicals are treated as annuals in cold climates.) All have a long blooming season, and once set in a still-water pool with at least five hours sun and fertile soil, they are no trouble—there is no weeding or watering. In a small aquarium indoors, try the miniature Margaret Mary.

PERENNIAL garden above features summer phlox. Try today's hybrids. You will be surprised at the glorious colors. There is nothing in these even remotely resembling the half-wild magenta phlox seen in abandoned gardens. Try interplanting summer phlox with bearded iris, peonies, daylilies, hardy asters, and chrysanthemums for blooms all season.

111

POCKETS for planting bring order to the garden and show off plants to great advantage. A piece of flagstone left out of the terrace, above, opens the way for a clump of pansies and spuria iris. After hot weather arrives the pansies can be replaced with any low-growing flower such as ageratum, alyssum, or dwarf geranium. Redwood triangles, upper right, rest on timbers used as risers for the concrete patio block steps. Plants include gerbera daisies, gray-carpeting cerastium, sedums, sempervivums, and echeverias. Redwood outlines pockets, lower right. Try low-growing annuals for quick cover in pockets: petunias, portulaca, verbena, and dwarf zinnias.

Phil Fein

Maynard L. Parker

Gottscho-Schleisner

Paul E. Genereux

PRIMROSES are the most colorful of all spring-flowering hardy perennials. They thrive in moist soil, enriched with peat moss and leaf mold. Plants live longer if shaded in summer. With ample soil about the roots, and water, they transplant readily, even in full bloom. Use for bedding and in container gardens. *Primula denticulata* varieties bloom early bringing a moire of lavender, pink, rose, and white about six inches above the ground. Naturalize under high shade trees, or use in formal plantings with spring bulbs. These are followed by *Primula polyanthus* hybrids, shown opposite in the company of trilliums, in flowers of unmatched brilliance—blue, brown, burgundy, crimson, garnet, pink, white, and yellow. *P. acaulis* varieties bring other exciting colors, including apricot, bronze, claret, pink, and turquoise. Slightly later, *P. auricula* opens buds in such unusual flower colors as blue and green. The umbels of *P. sieboldi*, upper left, may be in white, rose, or purple, with individual flowers up to two inches across, in late spring. *P. japonica*, lower left, blooms in late spring and early summer, thrusting strong scapes 8 to 24 inches tall, in white, rose, lilac, maroon-red, striped white, white with crimson eye, and salmon. To have primroses in your spring garden, buy started plants in early spring, or early fall from a local or mail-order supplier, or, sow seeds in February and March for bloom the next year. For information about the American Primrose Society, write to 14015 Eighty-fourth Ave. N.E., Bothell, Wash.

Paul E. Genereux

PRIVACY is a scarce commodity in our crowded world and since man's territorial imperative seems to require a place to call his own, it is also much sought after. Privacy for a large open garden, above, is achieved by the artful use of both fence and high-growing shrubs. The intimate privacy of the patio, above right, results from both the structural details of the house and selective plantings. An entrance is cleverly screened from the world with golden bamboo, right.

Roger J. Sturtevant   Paul Peart

Jacobsen Manufacturing Company

PROBLEMS are solved most effectively when ingenuity is used to turn them into opportunities. A narrow, sun-drenched area, left, becomes a beauty spot when sun-loving perennials—peonies, lupines, rambler rose, a biennial edge of sweet William and petunias—are planted. Below, aerosol spray cans are quick and efficient solutions for the pests and diseases which attack house plants. Brick mowing strip used along the house, above, eliminates trimming and is an attractive border. Use along plant beds, fences, and walks. A utility area is hidden by the fence, right, which provides backdrop for a handsome apple espalier.

Gottscho-Schleisner

Gottscho-Schleisner

118

PROPAGATION by stem cuttings becomes an inexpensive and easy operation with the use of a plastic bag as a window-sill greenhouse. Try foliage plants, such as ivy, philodendron, and Chinese evergreen any time during the year; conifers, such as yew and juniper, in January and early February; garden flowers, such as geraniums, lantana, and roses from late May through August; flowering shrubs, such as forsythia, mock-orange, and viburnum from mid-June to mid-August; broadleaf evergreens, such as holly, azaleas, and camellias from mid-June to mid-August. (Left): To construct a plastic-bag greenhouse, screen brown fibrous peat moss through a quarter-inch wire mesh. Mix two parts of the peat to one part clean, salt-free sand. Mix thoroughly with water. Leave just enough water so that only a few drops of water can be squeezed out of a handful of the mixture. (Right): Place enough of the soil to make about four inches of firm rooting soil in a two-quart plastic freezer bag that has no holes in it. Pick a light green cutting about four to eight inches long for rooting. Cuttings are ready for rooting if, when broken, they snap like a fresh stringbean. Never take cuttings from growth that is soft and rubbery.

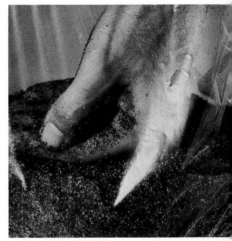

United States Department of Agriculture

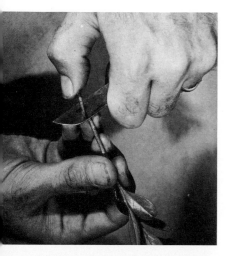

(Left): Remove the leaves from the lower third to half of the cutting. Make a straight cut across the base with a sharp knife. Then take a very thin sliver off the side of the cutting about an inch long ending at the base. Dip the end of the cutting in rooting hormone. Place the cutting two or three inches deep in the sand and peat mixture. Space cuttings so the leaves barely touch each other. Sprinkle them with just enough water to wet the foliage. (Right): Seal the top of the bag with a rubber band and place the "greenhouse" on a window sill which does not receive direct sun. Cuttings of most plants will root in eight to ten weeks. After eight weeks open the bag and remove a cutting. If a number of roots one-half to one inch long have formed, the cutting can be transplanted into a pot. Cuttings which have not rooted but are in good condition should be reset and inspected every two weeks. Before transplanting cuttings, condition them to a less humid atmosphere by gradually opening the bag over a five- to seven-day period. During this time, be sure to keep the original moisture content of the rooting soil.

121

PROPAGATION by air-layering has been prac-
ticed for centuries on the figs, and plants such
as the dieffenbachia, croton, oleander, and dra-
caenas. However, the application of plastic films
to this kind of reproduction is a recent innova-
tion which eliminates the need for constant attention. When your plants become unsightly as
with this fiddleleaf fig, far left, it's time to try air-
layering. New roots can be formed along the stem,
and the bottom of the plant removed by the use
of the air-layering technique. Make a one-inch
slanting cut to about the depth of one-half the
diameter of the plant. Hold the wound open
with a toothpick or match. Apply a rooting hormone to the open wound. Saturate a handful of
sphagnum moss with water and squeeze it dry.
Wrap the damp sphagnum around the wounded
area and force a small quantity up into the cut
portion. Wrap a sheet of plastic around the ball
of sphagnum. Use the polyethylene film from
frozen fruits or vegetables since this type prevents
drying of the moss but allows for the exchange
of air. Tie or tape each end of the plastic. Ex-
amine the plant occasionally without removing
the plastic to see when the roots are forming.
When the roots are the size shown, remove the
plastic and the plant will be ready for potting.
Cut the newly rooted plant off just below the
mass of roots. Pot in a container large enough to
accommodate the root system and watch it grow.

Iowa State University

Maynard L. Parker

PRUNING is such a necessity in keeping up the garden, we forget it can also be an art.

Clipping and bending the right twigs at the right time produced the container-grown

espalier, above, with modified "poodle" cut. Result: a piece of living sculpture.

PRUNING is the art behind training bushy plants to tree form, like the coleus, below.

Start with rooted cutting. Add stake. Remove sideshoots as soon as they start. At desired height remove tip to begin tree head. Pinch out branch tips as they form.

Roche

Gottscho-Schleisner

Quick color goes in containers, opposite, as polyanthus primroses in full bloom are planted in redwood boxes. When hot weather arrives, these perennials can be planted in a cool, shaded, moist part of the garden to recuperate for next spring's bloom. Replace with containers of hybrid petunias, geraniums, White Bedder nicotiana, and marigolds. Quick patio, above, is borrowed from the art of the flowershow maker: a plan drawn to scale and all materials on hand at the time they are needed— gravel and flagstones, sod, evergreens, a clump birch, garden bench, and seasonal flowers. Hard work for a day, but the closest thing to an instant patio with permanent appeal. Quick shade is given by the castor-bean plant, right, which shoots up from seed to eight feet or more in the first weeks of summer.

Gottscho-Schleisner

RENOVATING an old garden requires that you carefully evaluate what you have and what you want to have. Start by indicating accurately on scale paper the placement of all major trees, shrubbery borders, flower beds, outdoor living areas, paved surfaces, and buildings on your property. Using a piece of tracing paper, take from the master plan everything you want or have to keep. Transfer this information to a clean sheet of scale paper. Add new plant materials, paved areas, and structures such as a swimming pool or storage shed. When you have a plan you think will work, try putting it into three-dimensional form, like the scale-model landscape shown above. This will enable you to have a near-perfect plan before any physical labor or expense has been incurred. (A good winter project.) Majestic shade trees form a leafy canopy over the outdoor living room, opposite, where the usual lawn and flower beds had become difficult to maintain in competition with trees for water, light, and food. Grass, creeping veronica, or mazus, between paving stones is easy to keep up by feeding with liquid fertilizer occasionally through the growing season. Container plants thrive on light feedings weekly. Oleanders and lantanas trained to tree form stand on either side of the entry. Pots of petunias, geraniums, and hydrangeas decorate the area.

RENOVATING an old garden can adapt it to a different generation or simply to fit your own life-style. One gardener may love rows on rows of rose beds with manicured grass walkways. To another this would be a high-maintenance trap. Redwood garden house and pool, above, have a no-maintenance setting of ground covers and gravel. New garden for an old house, opposite, uses a rustic arbor to support gnarled wisteria. Beyond, an Oriental garden where may be found bamboo, boulders, azaleas, a stone lantern, and statue arranged to represent the timeless beauties of nature.

RESTORING once beautiful gardens to their former splendor has been part of the work at Colonial Williamsburg in Virginia since 1926. Like the furniture inside the houses, these eighteenth-century gardens are worthy of being copied and cultivated as today's surrounds for living outdoors. The Powell-Waller garden, above, is tightly designed in geometric forms. Boxwood and holly are used extensively and color is added by tulips, dogwood, and Cherokee roses. At the Palmer house, upper right, a boxwood garden grows in brick-outlined pattern with gravel walks and sun dial. Try re-creating a classic garden like the one lower right, if you have a suitable site. Marble chips make an elegant carpet for designs in clipped boxwood or privet.

Colonial Williamsburg

Gottscho-Schleisner

ROCK gardens in vertical form give a place to grow and display trailing plants to great advantage. The important thing is to keep them thinned out sufficiently to reveal the character of the rock wall. In the dry-wall garden above, creeping phlox, basket-of-gold alyssum, and perennial candytuft are at the peak of spring bloom. There will be sedums, campanulas, and an array of pinks (dianthus species) in summer.

An unusual rockery plant to try is *Androsace lanuginosa*, left, which opens clusters of white flowers, brushed with pink, from June to October, on trailing plants with silvery leaves.

Home Garden

134

Roche

ROCK gardens duplicate swatches of an alpine meadow. The planting above features a small stream, and a place to grow *Epigaea repens, Primula sieboldi,* dwarf evergreens, astilbe, violets, ferns, and mosses. Plant a rock garden around natural outcroppings of stones and boulders, or build one using sandstone, waterworn limestone, or lightweight Featherock® (check Yellow Pages for a local dealer).

The fragrant netted iris, right, blooms early nestled in a planting pocket between two boulders. *Saxifraga sarmentosa,* the popular houseplant "strawberry-begonia" which is also winter hardy outdoors, carpets the ground.

Home Garden

135

Jacobsen Manufacturing Company

ROOFTOP gardens like the one above are especially delightful because they are so unexpected. Visitors and cliff-dwellers alike find the existence of lush foliage and fragrant flowers in miraculous contrast with granite canyons. On a rooftop try quick-growing trees and vines. Use containers of bright annuals in a strong color scheme. Feed weekly. Water as often as necessary to keep soil moist at all times. Roof drip line, left, can be eliminated by using a gravel strip in area where plants and lawn fail to grow. Roof overhang, opposite, provides a place to hang baskets of fuchsias. Also note what can be done in a narrow side yard by organizing space.

Gottscho-Schleisner

ROSE garden framed by clipped hedge of dwarf yew, above, receives a half day of sun, which is ample for sturdy growth, yet not so much that delicate colors are bleached prematurely. Everblooming hybrid teas are used with tree roses for accent. If you share the popular feeling that roses should be fragrant, the modern variety Lemon Spice, right, will be welcome in your garden. *Rosa wichuraiana*, the

Armstrong Nurseries

memorial rose, opposite, yields single flowers in pink, red, or white. It is semievergreen and spreads rapidly by canes that take root, forming a rugged ground cover for steep banks and rocky slopes. As shown here it spills over the top of a brick retaining wall. For information about the American Rose Society write to 4048 Roselea Place, Columbus, Ohio 43214. Dues include magazine and yearbook.

Gottscho-Schleisner   Paul E. Genereux

ROSES thrive in seaside garden, above, surrounded by border of astilbe, pyrethrum, heuchera, foxglove, campanula, and delphinium. Roses are unequaled for formal plantings, large or small. Walled garden, right, features hybrid tea, grandiflora, and rambler roses with lilies, delphinium, clematis, yew espalier, clipped dwarf euonymus hedge, bench, and sun dial. Polyanthus roses grow in cutting garden opposite, edged early in season by pansies. Grapestake fence, redwood edging for bed, and bricks give contemporary feeling to garden. Try arranging roses with strawberries (both belong to apple family) with littleleaf holly in berry basket, below.

Larry B. Nicholson

Gottscho-Schleisner

SEASIDE garden that meets the Atlantic, opposite upper, shows distinct belts of exposure to salt spray. Beach grass grows in sparse clumps near the water. Farther back it thrives, and serves to give stability to shifting dunes. Still more inland, inside a picket fence that shields young plants from spring winds, annual flowers thrive in the bracing atmosphere, producing colors of unmatched brilliance. Trees in foreground have been contorted into fantasy shapes by years of strong wind and salt spray. Redwood deck and zigzag seating area, opposite lower, serve as an inviting easy-upkeep surface for relaxing and entertaining at the edge of the Pacific. Prostrate junipers and lavender (in bloom) grow in serpentine-curved beds with tree roses for accent.

SHADE from towering old tree, right, gives an ideal place to grow a collection of tuberous-rooted begonia hybrids. These tender bulbs need an early start indoors as for caladiums (pages 38–39). A growing mixture rich in well-rotted leaf mold, and biweekly feeding with an organic fish fertilizer will produce amazing results; individual flowers measure up to eight inches or more in diameter. Basket types may be hung from tree branches, or roof overhang. As soon as they are large enough to nip out, it is a good idea to remove the first flower buds of the season; this is necessary only for two or three weeks to give the root system ample time to develop.

Roche

SHADE is a positive factor to deal with in the garden. The right plants will thrive in it. You simply work with a different repertory than you would in a sunny area. Shade may be partial, dappled, light, high, deep, or gloomy. With the right plant materials, it can always be a welcome place where light is pleasant to the eyes and summer temperatures are noticeably lower. Large trees and shrubs compete for moisture and plant food. Enrich the soil with peat moss or well-rotted compost. Water deeply during times of drought. Bold shapes, opposite, etch an inviting picture in this shaded garden where delicate epimediums carpet the ground around azaleas and rhododendrons. Fountains of daylily foliage send up buds that open to light the shade with pale lemon blooms. Lavender hosta flowers rise from the large clumps of glaucous, quilted leaves that catch the light all season. Forget-me-nots and violets edge the lily pool. A rocky stair leads to earthenware container which on occasion may hold feathery plumes of pampas grass, an armful of September asters, or Joe pye weed. Where grass would be a problem in a shaded back yard, upper right, a patch of wild flowers grows beautifully as if deep in the woods. Mountain-laurel gives spring flowers, green foliage all year. April and May bring ladyslippers, woods phlox, tiny alpine columbine, violets, lily of the valley, trilliums, and tiarella. Ferns offer a cooling cover in summer. Man-made shade, lower right, gives an immediate place to grow shade-loving plants where trees cannot or do not exist.

SHELVES added to fence turn it into a display and growing area for choice small potted plants during warm weather. Site receives bright light all day, full sun early in the morning. Young house plants summered this way make a much more interesting show than when they are set on the ground outdoors, but they do require watering once and sometimes twice a day. Biweekly feeding with liquid fertilizer will keep growth prospering, and many will require repotting by midsummer. Kinds shown above include aloe, fittonia, rex begonia, cacti, apple geranium, English ivy, citrus, podocarpus, polyscias, and pedilanthus.

SHRUB borders that have grown tall, thick, and ungainly, can be updated by thinning, removing all dead wood, and underplanting with choice low-growing plants. In the foundation planting, left, old lilacs and deciduous azaleas have been saved, and underplanted with dwarf yew, pieris, and other evergreens. Euonymus forms attractive hedge; redwood edges beds and weathered bricks complete the pleasing new-old contrast. Foundation planting, below, features rhododendrons, azaleas, and daffodils for spring bloom. Try a border of shrubs designed to bring year-round color to the garden. For greatest effect keep simultaneous bloomers in groups rather than scattered.

Paul E. Genereux

STANDARDS bring old world charm to contemporary gardens. Try training a favorite bushy plant to tree form. Use a geranium, heliotrope, fuchsia, tibouchina, gardenia, or coleus. Shown in garden at left are hybrid tea roses with boxwood, tulips. Handsome lantana trees, above, grow in terracotta tubs as accents for all-green boxwood garden. Tree lilac (*Syringa palibiniana*) is hardiest standard.

Paul E. Genereux

Jeannette Grossman

STEPS outdoors should ramble more gently than those inside. When building garden steps, work with an eye for both attractive design and safety. The width should be in proportion to the location, but they must also permit comfortable and safe passage. Generally, the longer the flight of steps, the wider it should be. The horizontal surface or tread should be at least 12 inches wide and the vertical or front wall 7 inches or less. Materials used in constructing steps can either blend or contrast with other materials already existing in the garden. Pebbles are used, upper right, to cover an odd-shaped strip of ground between steps of quarried stone, and the edge of a new terrace. They make a pleasant

Phil Fein

150

transition and are repeated as ground cover in a plant bed beyond the terrace. A generous curve will add interest to a long flight of stairs. Curves can also provide a wide landing for a moment of rest for the climber. The winding woodland staircase, upper left, makes excellent use of the curve principle. The steps of railroad ties and concrete lead to a collection of flowering shrubs; clumps of astilbe are in full bloom. Ferns and black-eyed Susans mix to form a dense, country-casual edging. By contrast, the material and planting of the steps, lower left, work as a model of suburban formality. The exactness of the well-ordered brick in the steps and raised planting bed combine with pebble-surfaced concrete to form a clean-lined entry. Since steps are for climbing both day and night, the light at the left adds safety as well as design interest. Arriving guests will also appreciate that the well-placed fixture lights the house number. Gravel and weathered railroad ties, lower right, combine in a pleasant way with the woodsy feeling of *Scilla campanulata*. This combination of step materials could be used in almost any situation short of a completely formal one. Try it in a shaded garden with ferns and hostas; in burning sunlight with creeping thyme, sedums, and sempervivums tucked in here and there.

Paul Peart

151

STEPS are an important tool of garden landscaping. Since terracing of land can add dimension to small areas and interest to large ones, they are almost always present in well-designed gardens. The boulders placed as a rough stepway, left, were originally taken from another part of the garden when it was graded. The result is a staircase which appears wrought by nature. This approach is particularly effective in a wild garden. The concept is carried out with creeping sedum, euonymus, and epimedium and white violets in bloom.

The steps, right, are a study in contrast. Paving stones of unpolished white marble wind from a random-stone patio to a hidden area, thus creating the illusion of space in a tiny garden. The clean, smooth surface of the marble is accentuated by combining it with heavily textured Palos Verdes rock specimens and a border of dwarf ginger, pteris and holly ferns, and *Alsophila australis* fern with ground cover of wild strawberry and dichondra.

SUPPLIERS of plants, seeds, bulbs, and equipment for gardening appear on pages 190–191.

Ward Linton

Larry B. Nicholson

Ward Linton

Lord & Burnham

SUCCULENTS propagate easily from seeds, leaf cuttings, or by division. When you have enough, try a pattern planting like the one opposite upper: various echeverias with the scarlet flowers of kalanchoe in the background; bamboo outlines the bed. In a few pots try different sempervivums, opposite lower left, set off by white marble chips; display attractively where the symmetrical forms can be appreciated. Have you ever taken time to study the beauty of buds unfurling, like the ones opposite lower right on echeveria? After the flowers fade, carefully clip out the stems and the leaf rosettes will continue being attractive. SUN PORCH to greenhouse: Worth trying if you have a room you would like to turn into a conservatory without

the expense of a complete change. Use window greenhouses like the ones shown. If you are usually at home and have time, ventilation can be done manually. Otherwise, buy automatic vent openers and use in combination with heating units, all thermostatically controlled.

Gottscho-Schleisner

SURFACES add texture and the symmetry of geometrics to civilize the random beauty of the garden. This contrast can be used effectively to achieve a pleasing design. Rather than skirt the tree, upper left, with the usual evergreen ground covers, the joining of trunk to earth has been left exposed and a combination of creeping phlox and pebbles mixed with a casualness which is a perfect foil for the regimentation of the used brick of the terrace. Lightweight masonry blocks have been integrated into the entire landscape design of the semitropical garden, lower left. The blocks serve as ground cover, walks, and patio floor. The possible boredom of a large expanse of a uniform surface is alleviated by forming the blocks into several different patterns. Extensive use of hard surface materials reduces the areas of cultivation and is ideal for the easy-care garden. The union of plant and stone ground covers makes a dramatic effect. A rigid geometric with great style is formed, upper right by matched squares of slate separated by dichondra. Thyme could be used as an alternate in cold climates; it will scent the air when crushed underfoot. A setting worthy of an Aphrodite is created, lower right, by the use of unpolished white marble with dichondra and a border of strawberry ground cover. The quiet mystery of this jewel-like patio is completed with a backdrop of pteris fern, holly fern, dicksonia fern, ophiopogon, clivias, and rhododendrons.

Paul Peart   Ward Linton

156

SURFACES can bring a new dimension to landscaping schemes. The garden, right, is a study in texture. Excitement of line and surface is everywhere. Concrete studded with smooth stones is separated from oversized, rough brick by plantings of creeping thyme and succulents. A symmetrical walk of glazed brick curves out of sight. In the patio, above, smooth and irregular-pebbled squares contrast for rustic sophistication.

Maynard L. Parker

SURFACES with originality: Nothing commonplace about pebbled concrete when six circles are placed in the corner, upper left. Mondrian-like effect is created by using grass instead of concrete squares in the walk, lower left. Surprise visitors by edging patio squares with colorful pebbles, above.

George de Gennaro

161

SURPRISE flower for fall, winter, or spring is the camellia, right. Not so surprising that it blooms, perhaps, but that the flowers of such amazing symmetry, perfection, and delicacy grow on a plant so easily cultivated. Try camellias outdoors if they survive your winters; otherwise, grow them in containers which can be kept outdoors in a shady place in summer, indoors in cold weather.

George W. Park Seed Company

SURPRISE for spring: Try massing one variety of bulb in a sweep of color. Plant thickly. The patriotic theme above uses double early red tulips, blue muscari (grape-hyacinths), and white daffodils.

SURPRISING coolness is given by a fountain on a hot day. In the garden above, potted shrubs and cyclamen accent the pebble mosaic surface. If traffic or other noise is annoying in your garden, try masking it with the pleasant splashing sound of water.

162

SURPRISE vine for summer and autumn color is the clematis. Hybrids like the one above give great bursts of bloom off and on from late spring until severe freezing in the fall. Even in cold climates you may find a few clematis flowers to cut for a Thanksgiving arrangement. Many kinds have fascinating seedheads which may be cut through the winter. For a real surprise, try growing clematis as a winter pot plant in a sunny, moist, cool window or greenhouse.

SURPRISING summer bulb *Lycoris squamigera*, far left, opens bouquets of fragrant, lavender-pink flowers in August. These blossoms crown bare stems that thrust out of the earth with sudden urgency in late July. Leaves appear in spring, die in midsummer. Plant in early fall. Ornamental alliums, like A. *karataviense*, near left, bloom from May to July, depending on variety. A. *giganteum* is spectacular with huge heads of violet flowers atop four-foot stems. By contrast, A. *ostrowskianum* grows only six inches tall. Plant bulbs in spring or fall. Hardy *Begonia evansiana*, below, has red-veined green leaves and pink flowers. Try it for summer color in shade; plant in sandy, moist leaf mold. Mulched lightly, it survives northern winters outdoors.

Paul Kohl

165

SURPRISING bulbs—here are six of unusual interest to plant outdoors in the spring for summer color, or in a sunny window or greenhouse for winter flowers. Tigridias, left, open new flowers every day all summer. Store corms over winter, as gladiolus. Try keeping amaryllis dormant in winter; plant outdoors in spring for garden color, lower left. Montbretia, below, grows easily through the fall and winter for blooms in a home greenhouse: Try it, along with the related ixia. Rare blue amaryllis, *Worsleya rayneri*, near right, keeps green foliage all year. Try it from seeds, as other amaryllis. The climbing lily, *Gloriosa rothschildiana*, far upper right, needs rich, moist soil, and dappled sun. Unusual irid, the homeria, far

George W. Park Seed Company

lower right, has only recently come into circulation. Try it outdoors as a gladiolus; indoors as a montbretia or freesia.

TOPIARY is a rewarding garden art form, but it takes years of patient development. The upkeep never stops. Plants used include boxwood, yew, and privet; to a lesser extent juniper and arbor-vitae; rosemary for miniature work; and *Laurus nobilis* in the South. Topiary is the clipping, pruning, and training of a plant to a geometric or animal shape. The peacock topiary, left, stands watch over a terrace, with trees forming a leafy backdrop; tulips and azaleas bloom in the spring with a low, clipped boxwood hedge. Boxwood topiaries are a highlight of the gardens at Colonial Williamsburg, upper right, where they serve as accents among precision-trimmed hedges and parterre plots filled with spring bulbs and pansies; budded lilies and hollyhocks promise later bloom. Magnificent old shade trees grow in background.

TREES are for cooling shade, warming windbreak, flowers, fruit, showy berries, and sometimes a place to hang a swing, build a lofty house, or to climb. In a shade tree you want a kind that will grow well where you live, but not so well that it is weedy; one that leafs out early and holds leaves late in the fall; one that is deep-rooted so that you can garden beneath it; and one that is resistant to pest and disease. Ask your neighbors and local nurserymen the kinds they recommend in your area. Flowering trees like the dogwood, lower right, add beauty to the landscape and give light shade.

168   *Gottscho-Schleisner*

TULIPS give six weeks of nonstop bloom in spring gardens. Earliest are the "botanicals," many of which have recently been extensively hybridized. *Tulipa tarda* or *T. dasystemon*, below center, opens three to six blooms on each six-inch stem; Persian Gem is similar, but nearly all-gold. Plant and leave undisturbed; ideal in rockery. Hybrids of *T. kaufmanniana*, the water-lily tulip, below right, bloom with the daffodils; six to eight inches tall. Drift at the front of a border, or in a rock garden. Bouquet tulip Plum Purty, below, opens five or six blooms on each 28-inch branched stem. May-flowering Darwin, cottage, and breeder varieties, right, complete the tulip season.

George W. Park Seed Company

Ward Linton

VEGETABLES can be beautiful. The secret lies in the way they are planted and maintained. Some kinds, like the redhot pepper, upper left, are so ornamental that any utilitarian use seems quite secondary. Tomatoes join this category when they are artfully espaliered on a sunny wall or trellis. Two exceedingly showy vegetables to try: flowering kale and ornamental cabbage. Planting pockets in patio, above, hold leaf lettuce and radishes for salads; ferny carrot leaves are decorative until harvested. Boxwood frames vegetable garden of ultimate beauty, left, with tomatoes trained teepee-style, basil, and a few flowers. Roses for cutting grow in adjacent bed.

Maynard L. Parker

VINES to carpet and drape the garden: Polka Dot vinca, above left. Baskets of white star-of-Bethlehem and blue lobelia, above right, with astilbe flowering in boxes underneath. Opposite, clockwise beginning upper left: Yellow flowered Allamanda for house or greenhouse. Basket of gold alyssum for rockery. Clematis hybrids Mme. Le Coultre and Mrs. P. B. Truax. Wisteria is espaliered on patio interior wall.

George W. Park Seed Company

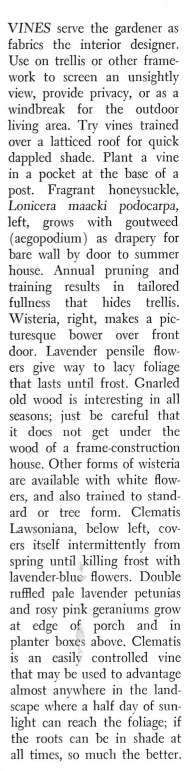

VINES serve the gardener as fabrics the interior designer. Use on trellis or other framework to screen an unsightly view, provide privacy, or as a windbreak for the outdoor living area. Try vines trained over a latticed roof for quick dappled shade. Plant a vine in a pocket at the base of a post. Fragrant honeysuckle, *Lonicera maacki podocarpa*, left, grows with goutweed (aegopodium) as drapery for bare wall by door to summer house. Annual pruning and training results in tailored fullness that hides trellis. Wisteria, right, makes a picturesque bower over front door. Lavender pensile flowers give way to lacy foliage that lasts until frost. Gnarled old wood is interesting in all seasons; just be careful that it does not get under the wood of a frame-construction house. Other forms of wisteria are available with white flowers, and also trained to standard or tree form. Clematis Lawsoniana, below left, covers itself intermittently from spring until killing frost with lavender-blue flowers. Double ruffled pale lavender petunias and rosy pink geraniums grow at edge of porch and in planter boxes above. Clematis is an easily controlled vine that may be used to advantage almost anywhere in the landscape where a half day of sunlight can reach the foliage; if the roots can be in shade at all times, so much the better.

W ATER is refreshing to see and hear in a garden, and while it may not actually lower the temperature on a hot day, at least it makes you feel cooler. The lily and goldfish pool, above, has three depths: water-lilies and lotus thrive at 24 inches deep; arrowhead and arum-lily grow at 12 inches; and sweet flag, marsh marigold, and the water forget-me-not are planted at the 6-inch depth. Water-hyacinths float among the lily pads, and oxygenating myriophyllum and elodea live underwater. A simple reflecting pool, below, molded from wet concrete makes special a corner of the garden, a place where birds and small animals come for a drink. Surrounding plants are small-scale also: alpine strawberries, sweet alyssum, and miniature columbine. A hidden recirculating pump takes water from the pool, opposite, and sends it splashing back over rocks. Surrounding plants include ferns, cyperus, forget-me-not, marsh marigold, primula, rock cotoneaster, violets, candytuft, rhododendron, columbine, and tiarella.

Paul Peart

WATER used in the garden is the undisputed province of the Japanese. The classic Japanese garden, upper left, is a bird-watcher's delight. Water splashes in a metal container above a clear reflecting pool. Textures and materials are mixed deftly in the simple, understated garden, lower left. The Oriental influence is accentuated by using concrete slabs planted with ivy as sculpture. The reflecting pool, above, becomes purely Occidental when placed in a bed of spring flowers: doronicum, bellis, primroses, basket of gold alyssum, pansies, and grape-hyacinths.

WATER garden at edge of a patio, opposite, is lighted at night to reveal goldfish and exotic lilies that bloom in the evening. Next to pool, by wall, is a place to grow plants that need abundant moisture: arrowhead, marsh marigold, primulas, and Japanese iris. Baby's-breath, dwarf azalea, and bluebell campanula grow in planting pockets hollowed out of flagstone surface. A little wild garden, above, allows escape from the implied regimentation of the formally organized landscape that surrounds. Low-maintenance and simple pleasure guide the planting. In early spring this area is sunny until the trees leaf out, and random clumps of narcissus, species tulips, and other bulbs burst into bloom. Later mazus, sedum, violets, and ferns grow congenially, forming a moire of refreshing greens. For natural stepping stones in a wild garden, try redwood rounds, shown at right with festuca tufts.

Ward Linton

WILDERNESS garden at Colonial Williamsburg, below, features naturalized tulips, narcissus, and *Phlox divaricata*. Woodsy, wild garden, below right, suggests what can be done with a steep bank. Choice wild flowers and ferns grow with dwarf rhododendrons, evergreens, and dogwood.

Colonial Williamsburg

WILD FLOWERS in spring, a meadow in summer, above: Clusiana tulips, mertensia, primroses, daffodils, rhododendrons bloom under dogwood.

Maynard L. Parker

WILD, in a restrained way, is this little retreat in the city, an appletree garden where ferns, violets, woodland lilies, hostas, iris, and tuberous begonias grow in dappled shade. Simple brick path provides easy access to the planting beds, and leads to statue.

WINTER'S most splendid luxury for a gardener is a greenhouse attached to the house, opposite. Invest in a prefabricated model equipped with automatic controls. You will be pleasantly surprised to find this is one product that is still reasonably priced. If you have no space for a regular greenhouse, install a window greenhouse, opposite lower. Where severe cold is a problem, small electric heaters can be used. If you are out of the house in the daytime, use automatic vent motors which will provide fresh air as needed through the day to keep the greenhouse in a predetermined temperature range. Plants shown include wax begonias, cyperus, creeping fig, oxalis, columnea, philodendron, begonias, polyscias, ferns, episcias, bromeliads, and orchids. There aren't many flowers that bloom in the winter outdoors, but the Christmas rose, *Helleborus niger*, above with snowberries, blooms in any period of mild weather that amounts to a "February thaw." For more bloom, situate in a sun pocket, protected from wind, ice, and deep snowdrifts. Helleborus thrives in deep, rich, moist, leaf mold.

WINTER will be nicer for the birds if you make them a holiday wreath from evergreen clippings (cedar shown, left), decorated with suet cups, nut meats, and rosehips. Replenish the feast, either on the wreath, or in a feeder, as needed until spring.

Larry B. Nicholson

WINTER is a good time to organize all the handy and necessary tools that go with gardening. Tools kept in the right place, always clean and ready to use, add immeasurably to the pleasures of gardening. Pegboard, opposite, is easily mounted on any wall, and with hardware designed for the purpose, quickly provides a place for every tool. Clean and oil all metal parts before storing tools for the winter. Paint handles in bright colors to make lost tools more easily detected in the garden.

WINTER snow will seem to melt into drifts of flowers in the spring if you sow seeds of hardy annuals around Christmas time. Simply broadcast the seeds over the area where you want bloom. If there is snow on the ground, so much the better; seeds nestled in the snow will eventually come to rest on the soil surface, to sprout and grow sturdily in the first warm days of spring. Some seeds sown this way will be eaten by the birds, others carried away by rain and wind, so plant generously. If you are sowing in the absence of snow cover, scatter the seeds under frosted plants of annuals and perennials, which will be removed in early spring. Favorite annual flowers for winter sowing include larkspur, California and Shirley poppies, right, bachelor's-button, nemophila, nigella, candytuft, and godetia. All are excellent to broadcast over beds of spring bulbs.

Paul E. Genereux

SUPPLIERS

Suppliers of plants, seeds, bulbs, and equipment for gardening:
(If charge is made for catalog, price is indicated.)

Abbot's Nursery, Route 4, Box 482, Mobile, Alabama 36609—*Camellias.*

Alpenglow Gardens, 13328 King George Highway, North Surrey, B.C., Canada—*Alpine plants.*

Aluminum Greenhouses, 14615 Lorain Ave., Cleveland, Ohio 44111—*Prefabricated greenhouses.*

Antonelli Brothers, 2545 Capitola Rd., Santa Cruz, California—*Tuberous begonias, gloxinias.*

Warren and Susan Baldsiefen, Box 88, Bellvale, New York 10912 ($1)—*Rhododendrons.*

Claude A. Barr, Prairie Gem Ranch, Smithwick, South Dakota 57782—*Wild flowers.*

Beahm Gardens, 2686 East Paloma St., Pasadena, California 91107—*Orchid cacti.*

Bountiful Ridge Nurseries, Princess Anne, Maryland 21853—*General nursery stock.*

Brand Peony Farms, Box 36, Faribault, Minnesota 55021.

Bristol Nurseries, Bristol, Connecticut —*Hardy chrysanthemums.*

Brown's Sunnyhill Gardens, Route 4, Box 136, Walla Walla, Washington 99362—*Iris.*

Albert H. Buell Greenhouses, Eastford, Connecticut ($1)—*Gloxinias, African violets, other gesneriads.*

Burgess Seed and Plant Co., Galesburg, Michigan 49053—*General seed and nursery.*

W. Atlee Burpee Co., Philadelphia, Pennsylvania 19132—*General seed, bulb, and supplies.*

Caprilands Herb Farm, Coventry, Connecticut (Postage).

The Conard-Pyle Co., Star Roses, West Grove, Pennsylvania.

Cook's Geranium Nursery, Lyons, Kansas 67554 (25¢).

Cooley's Gardens, Silverton, Oregon 97381 (50¢)—*Iris.*

The Daffodil Mart, Gloucester, Virginia 23061.

De Jager and Sons, Inc., 188 Asbury St., South Hamilton, Massachusetts 01982—*All kinds of bulbs.*

Henry Field Seed and Nursery Co., Shenandoah, Iowa 51601—*General seed and nursery.*

Fischer Greenhouses, Linwood, New Jersey 08221—*African violets.*

Gardens of the Blue Ridge, Ashford, McDowell County, North Carolina 28603—*Wild flowers.*

Gardenside Nurseries, Inc., Shelburne, Vermont 05482—*Hardy bulbs.*

Girard Nurseries, North Ridge East, RD 4, Geneva, Ohio 44041—*Trees and shrubs.*

Hilltop Herb Farms, Box 866, Cleveland, Texas 77327—*Herbs and house plants.*

Iris Test Gardens, Yakima, Washington —*Iris.*

Jackson and Perkins, 415 Riverside, Newport Beach, Calif. 92660—*Roses.*

Johnson Cactus Gardens, Box 458, Paramount, Cailfornia 90723 (25¢).

Michael Kartuz Greenhouses, 92 Chestnut St., Wilmington, Massachusetts (25¢)—*Rare house plants.*

Joseph J. Kern Rose Nursery, Box 33, Mentor, Ohio 44060—*Old roses.*

Krider Nurseries, Inc., Middlebury, Indiana 46540—*General nursery.*

Lamb Nurseries, East 101 Sharp Ave., Spokane, Washington 99202—*Hardy perennials.*

Lins Glad and Peony Farm, Cologne, Minnesota 55322 (50¢).

Logee's Greenhouses, 55 North St., Danielson, Connecticut 06239—*Rare house plants.*

Lord and Burnham, Irvington, New York 10533—*Home greenhouses.*

MacPherson Gardens, 2920 Starr, Oregon, Ohio 43616—*Hardy sempervivums.*

Walter Marx Gardens, Boring, Oregon 97009 (50¢)—*Japanese iris, hardy bulbs, lilies.*

Rod McLellan Co., 1450 El Camino Real, South San Francisco, California—*Orchids*.

Melrose Gardens, Route 1, Box 466, Stockton, California 95201 (25¢) —*Unusual iris*.

Merry Gardens, Camden, Maine 04843 (50¢)—*Rare house plants*.

Middlepen Plantation, P.O. Box 85, Orangeburg, South Carolina 29115 —*Tender bulbs*.

Mini-Roses, Station A, P.O. Box 4255, Dallas, Texas 75208—*Miniature roses*.

Musser Forests, Inc., Indiana, Pennsylvania—*Evergreens*.

Oakhill Gardens, Route 3, Box 87, Dallas, Oregon 97338—*Sedums and sempervivums*.

Oakhurst Gardens, P.O. Box 444, Arcadia, California 91006 (50¢)— *Unusual house plants; especially tender bulbs*.

George W. Park Seed Co., Greenwood, South Carolina 29646—*General seed, nursery, and supply firm*.

Parry Nurseries, Signal Mountain, Tennessee 37377—*Daylilies*.

Plantamation, Inc., 136 East 57 St., New York, N.Y. 10022—*Automatic watering devices for plants*.

Rayner Bros., Inc., Salisbury, Maryland 21801—*General nursery*.

G. C. Robbinson, 56 North Georgia Ave., Mobile, Alabama 36604— *Camellias*.

S. Scherer & Sons, 104 Waterside Rd., Northport, New York 11768 (25¢) —*Water plants*.

Schreiner's Gardens, Route 2, Box 297, Salem, Oregon 97308 (50¢) – *Iris*.

Sequoia Nurseries, 2519 E. Noble, Visalia, California—*Miniature roses*.

R. H. Shumway Seedsman, Rockford, Illinois 61101—*General seeds*.

C. G. Simon Nursery Co., P.O. Box 2873, Lafayette, Louisiana 70501 —*Daylilies*.

Sky-Cleft Gardens, Camp Street Ext., Barre, Vermont 05641 (10¢)— *Hardy perennials*.

Louis Smirnow, 85 Linden Lane, Brookville, New York 11545—*Peonies*.

Spring Hill Nurseries Co., Tipp City, Ohio 45371—*General nursery*.

Stark Brothers' Nurseries and Orchards Co., Louisiana, Missouri 63353 – *General nursery*.

Fred A. Stewart, Inc., 8606 East Las Tunas Dr., San Gabriel, California 91776—*Orchids*.

Sturdi-Built Mfg. Co., 11304 S. W. Boones Ferry Rd., Portland, Oregon 97219—*Home greenhouses*.

Sunnyslope Gardens, 8638 Huntington Dr., San Gabriel, California 91775 —*Unusual and fancy chrysanthemums*.

Thompson & Morgan, Ltd., Ipswich, England (25¢)—*General and rare seeds*.

Thon's Garden Mums, 25 West Golf Rd., Arlington Heights, Illinois 60005—*Hardy chrysanthemums*.

Three Springs Fisheries, Inc., Lilypons, Maryland 21717—*Water plants*.

Thurman's Gardens, Route 2, Box 259, Spokane, Washington 99207 (50¢) —*Hardy perennials*.

Tillotson's Roses, Brown's Valley Rd., Watsonville, California 95076 ($1)—*Old Roses*.

Tinari Greenhouses, 2325 Valley Rd., Huntingdon Valley, Pennsylvania 19006—*African violets*.

University Hills Nursery, 470 Delgado Dr., Baton Rouge, Louisiana 70808 —*Tender bulbs*.

Wayside Gardens Co., Mentor, Ohio 44060 ($2)—*General nursery; hardy and tender bulbs*.

White Flower Farms, Litchfield, Connecticut ($1)—*General nursery; hardy and tender bulbs*.

Gilbert H. Wild and Son, Inc., Sarcoxie, Missouri (50¢)—*Peonies, iris, daylilies*.

Wilson Bros., Roachdale, Indiana— *Geraniums, house plants*.

Thomas M. Wood, Constantia, New York 13044—*Wild flowers*.

Woodland Acres Nursery, Rt. 2, Crivitz, Wisconsin 54114—*Perennials*.

Melvin E. Wyant, Johnny Cake Ridge, Mentor, Ohio 44060 (25¢)— *Roses*.

INDEX

Greenhouses, 54, 55, 187; plastic-bag, 120–21; sun porch to, 155; window, 155, 187

Ground covers, 77–78 (see also specific plants); pebble, 150–51; in planting pockets, 77, 112; stone, 156; vine, 174

Hackberry tree, 47
Hawthorn, 22
Heather, 67, 69
Hedges, 80
Helenium, 29
Heliotrope, 149
Helleborus niger (Christmas rose), 109, 187
Heller Japanese holly, 26, 67
Herbs (herb garden), 64, 83. See also specific kinds of herbs
Here-and-now terrace, construction of, 104
Hesperis (sweet rocket), 23
Hibiscus, Chinese, 67, 87
Highbush cranberry, 22
Holly, 22, 67
Homeria, 166
Honeysuckle, 66, 71, 176
Horse chestnut tree, 47
Hosta, 145
Hunnemannia (Mexican tulip-poppy), 6
Hyacinths, 61
Hydrangeas, 29, 57, 80; hedges, 80

Iceland poppy, Champagne Bubbles hybrid, 6
Impatiens, 19, 58; dwarf-growing Elfin, 19
Indoor gardens, 84–87 (see also City gardens; Greenhouses); lights for, 95, 97; miniature plants for, 101
Iris, 107, 109, 135
Ismene, 35
Ivy: Algerian (variegated), 64; English, 43, 67, 78, 87

Jack's beanstalk garden, 42
Jade plants (crassula), 36
Japanese gardens, 88, 181
Japanese holly, 26, 67
Japanese maple trees, 60, 64
Japanese white pine, 26
Japanese yew, 67
Jasminum nudiflorum, 67
Juniper, 60, 67, 69, 77

Kale, 90, 173
Kohleria, 59
Korean grass, 78

Lamps. See Lights (lighting)
Landscaping, 90–96; borders, 29; city gardens, 47–48; decks, 63; decorations, 64; disappearing paths, 93; entry areas, 93; espaliers, 66, 67; evergreens, 68–69; fountains, 162; garden steps, 150–53; hedges, 80; lights (lighting), 95, 97; patios and terraces, 103–5, 127, 150–53; planting pockets, 112; privacy, 116, 176; problems, 118; renovating and restoring, 129–33; repetition and contrast techniques, 95; shade, 127, 143–45; surfaces, 156–61; topiary, 168; trees, 168; water, 178–83; vines (see Vines)

Lantana trees, 149
Larkspur, 189
Lemon tree, dwarfed, 44
Lemon verbena, 64
Liatris, 29
Lights (lighting), 95, 97
Lilac, 149
Lilies, 98–99; Aurelian, 98; Backhouse, 98; Black Dragon, 98; Croesus, 64; Enchantment, 64, 107; Harlequin, 98, 99; *L. auratum*, 98; *L. cernuum*, 99; *L. croceum*, 98; *L. japonicum*, 98; *L. rubellum*, 98; *L. speciosum*, 98; *L. szovitsianum*, 98; *L. tigrinum flaviflorum*, 98; Madonna, 29; Mid-Century, 98; Moonlight, 98; Paisley, 98; trumpets, 98; Turk's-cap, 99
Lily and goldfish pool, 178, 183
Linden tree, 47
Liriope, 66
Lobivopsis, Paramount hybrid, 36
Locust tree, 48
Lunaria (honesty or money plant), 23
Lupines, 29, 69, 118
Lycoris squamigera, 165

Madonna lilies, 29
Magnolia, star, 67
Maple trees, Japanese, 60, 64
Marantas, 87
Marigolds, 13, 60, 178, 183
Marsh marigold, 178, 183
Massagno asters, 10
Mesembryanthemum, 36
Mexican sunflower, 13
Mexican tulip-poppy, 6
Miniature plants, 101. See also Dwarfing plants (bonsai)
Mint, 64
Montbretia, 166
Morning glory, 42
Moso bamboo (*Phyllostachys edulis*), 16
Mountain-laurel, 145
Muscari (grape-hyacinths), 41, 162, 181
Myrtle, 27

Narcissus scaberulus, 101
Nemophila, 189

Solidago, 29
Sphagnum moss, 43, 123
Stachys, 64
Staircases, garden, 150–53
Standards, 149
Star magnolia, 67
Star roses, 101
Stem cuttings, propagation by, 120–22
Steps for gardens, 150–53, 183
Stone ground covers, 156, 158, 161. *See also* Pebbles
Strelitzia (Bird of Paradise), 25; *S. nicolai*, 25; *S. reginae*, 25
Succulents, 36, 57, 155 (see also specific kinds); carpeting, 78; miniature, 101
Sundial, armillary, 64
Sunflower, Mexican, 13
Sun porch to greenhouse, 155
Sunset cosmos, 6
Suppliers, garden equipment, 191–92
Surfaces, landscaping, 156–61
Sweet rocket (hesperis), 23
Sweet William, 23, 118
Sycamore tree, 47
Syringa palibiniana, 149

Terraces, 103–5
Terrarium, 31
Thyme, 64, 72, 78
Thymus serpyllum albus, 72
Tiger marigold, 13
Tigridias, 166
Tithonia, Fireball, 13
Tobacco, flowering (nicotiana), 9, 60
Tomatoes, 173
Tools, gardening, 189
Topiary, 168; children and, 43
Tradescantia fluminensis variegata, 19
Tree lilac, 149
Trees, 168 (see also specific kinds); citrus dwarfed, 44; dwarfing (bonsai), 26–27; flowering, 168; for city gardens, 47; ornamental fruit, 22; portable (container), 26–27, 60; shade, 129, 143, 168
Trilliums, 114

Tulip-poppy, Mexican, 6
Tulips, 170; Darwin, 170; double early red, 162; Persian Gem, 170; Plum Purty, 170; *T. dasystemon*, 170; *T. kaufmanniana*, 170; *T. tarda*, 170
Twinkles phlox, 11

Unguentine plant (*Aloe vera*), 41

Vegetable garden, 173
Verbascum, 23
Viburnums, 22; *V. opulus*, 22; *V. tomentosum*, 22; *V. trilobum* (highbush cranberry), 22; *V. xanthocarpum*, 22
Vines, 174–76 (see also specific kinds); for color, 163; for ground cover, 174
Violas, 23
Violet berries (beautyberry or callicarpa), 22
Violets, white, 153

Wallflower, 23
Wandering Jew, 19
Water (water garden), 178–83; for birds, 24; in Japanese garden, 88, 181
Water-hyacinths, 178
Watering pots, automatic, 16
Water-lilies, 111, 178; Margaret Mary miniature, 111
Weeping fig, 87
Wild flowers, 184
Wild garden, 183, 184, 185
Williamsburg, Va. *See* Colonial Williamsburg gardens
Willow tree, 47
Window greenhouses, 155, 187
Winged euonymus, 67
Winter: bird feeding, 188; garden plants, 187; seed sowing in, 189; tool care during, 189
Wisteria, 174, 176

Yellow-groove bamboo (*P. aureosulcata*), 16
Yew, 22, 147; Japanese dwarf, 67

Zinnias, 6, 9, 51, 53
Zoysia grass, 77